How to Cook Everything™

Everything™

Vege   oking

	DATE DUE		

Other Books by Mark Bittman:

How to Cook Everything™

How to Cook Everything™: Quick Cooking

How to Cook Everything™: Holiday Cooking

How to Cook Everything™: Easy Weekend Cooking

How to Cook Everything™: The Basics

The Minimalist Cooks at Home

The Minimalist Cooks Dinner

The Minimalist Entertains

Fish: The Complete Guide to Buying and Cooking

Leafy Greens

With Jean-Georges Vongerichten:

Simple to Spectacular

Jean-Georges: Cooking at Home with a Four-Star Chef

How to Cook
Everything™

Vegetarian Cooking

Mark Bittman

Illustrations by Alan Witschonke

WILEY

Wiley Publishing, Inc.

Published by Wiley Publishing, Inc., Hoboken, NJ

For general information on our other products and services or to obtain technical support please contact our Customer Care Department within the U.S. at 800-762-2974, outside the U.S. at 317-572-3993 or fax 317-572-4002.

Wiley also publishes its books in a variety of electronic formats. Some content that appears in print may not be available in electronic books.

Library of Congress Cataloging-in-Publication Data:

Bittman, Mark.

How to cook everything. Vegetarian cooking / Mark Bittman ;

illustrations by Alan Witschonke.

   p. cm.

ISBN 0-7645-2514-X (Paperback : alk. paper)

1. Vegetarian cookery. 2. Menus. I. Title.

TX837.B528 2003

641.5'636—dc21

           2003008740

Manufactured in the United States of America

10 9 8 7 6 5 4 3 2 1

Photos on pages xii, 12, 56, 86, and 102 © PhotoDisc, Inc. / Getty Images
Photo on page 38 © Corbis Digital Stock
Photos on pages 24 and 70 by David Bishop

For my parents and my kids

WILEY PUBLISHING, INC.

Publisher: Natalie Chapman

Executive Editor: Anne Ficklen

Senior Editor: Linda Ingroia

Production Editor: Ian Skinnari

Cover Design: Cecilia Diskin

Book Design: Edwin Kuo and Anthony Bagliani, Solid Design

Interior Layout: Holly Wittenberg

Manufacturing Buyer: Kevin Watt

Contents

Acknowledgments

I have been writing about food for nearly 25 years, and it's impossible to thank all the people who have helped me make a go of it during that time. Most of them know who they are—we have shared cooking, eating, and talking, much of what constitutes my life—and together I do owe them a broad "thanks."

However, some special friends and colleagues have been there for me and helped me out in recent years, and I want to thank them especially: Mitchell Orfuss, Naomi Glauberman, John Bancroft, Madeline Meacham, David Paskin, Pamela Hort, Jack Hitt, Semeon Tsalbins, Susan Moldow, Bill Shinker, Jim Nelson, Fred Zolna, Sherry Slade, Lisa Sanders, Genevieve Ko, Charlie Pinsky, Geof Drummond, Sam Sifton, Nancy Cobb, and Steve Rubin.

I have been blessed, too, with great colleagues at Wiley: Linda Ingroia, who has worked tirelessly on the new *How to Cook Everything* series; Edwin Kuo, Jeffrey Faust, Cecelia Diskin, and Holly Wittenberg for great covers and interiors; Ian Skinnari, the production editor, and Christina Van Camp for keeping keen eyes on clarity and consistency; and Kate Fischer and Michele Sewell for managing *How to Cook Everything* publicity opportunities. Jennifer Feldman got the *How to Cook Everything* series up and running and Natalie Chapman and Robert Garber have given it tremendous support. My agent, Angela Miller, is simply the best, and has been a terrific influence in my life for over a decade; huge thanks to her.

And, as always, special thanks to my fabulous children, Kate and Emma, and my most frequent companions, John H. Willoughby, John Ringwald, and Alisa X. Smith, all of whom give me invaluable love and perspective on a daily basis, and newfound confidence in the world of cooking.

I am not a nutritionist, dietitian, or even a vegetarian—far from it. But, like almost everyone else who cooks, I have seen the proportion of vegetables and grains in my diet grow steadily over the years, and—inadvertently or intentionally—there are a couple of days every week in which I eat no meat, poultry, or fish. Like most of the people who prefer never to eat those foods at all, I see such days as a little bit of being good for me and a little bit of being good for the planet, but mostly as an extension of "normal" that doesn't cause me to think about it much at all. Humans have long been, after all, omnivores, with a wide variety of diets based on what was available.

This, then, is a collection of my favorite, easy-to-use vegetarian recipes to help you enjoy vegetarian dinners, lunches, brunches, and snacks. (They can also be featured in meals that include meat; in fact, these recipes can be used in many different contexts, and not all of them need be exclusively vegetarian.) Almost all of the more than 90 recipes can be varied to your taste or diet, or what's available in your kitchen, so although this book is geared to a particular way of eating it is also a guide that can help you prepare any meal, and is a springboard for your creativity. There are dozens of variations, lists of quick flavoring ideas, and informal suggestions throughout the book. There are also tips to help you shop for, prepare, and cook the recipes, plus technique illustrations to help with the practical side of making them.

Although this book is not geared toward the completely dedicated vegetarian, you might want or need to know which recipes here are vegan—that is, made without dairy, eggs, or other animal products. This information can be useful if you're watching cholesterol intake, avoiding dairy in your diet, or just want to learn flavorful recipes with an emphasis on beans, grains, and vegetables, which tend to be highly valuable from a nutrition perspective. These vegan recipes are labeled with a **Ⓥ** icon. You'll also find that in many recipes, simply by replacing one ingredient—using oil instead of butter in Cabbage Braised with Onions (page 92), for example—the recipe becomes vegan.

If you're looking for vegetarian meal ideas, check the menus page in the back. You'll find 20 menus for weeknight, seasonal, special occasion, and healthful meals.

What to Know About Vegetarian Cooking

My basic belief about eating is the same as what dietitians have been saying for decades: Eat a wide variety of foods, all in moderation. We all have personal ways of defining "wide variety."

I eliminate almost nothing from my diet. Like most people I know, I try to "eat healthy" and, like most people I know, I don't always succeed. I know that food trends and dietary advice change all the time, and that the old joke from Woody Allen's movie *Sleeper* may turn out to be true—chocolate is the most important health food.

One bit of advice is so clear as to be inarguable, and that is that the more fruits, vegetables, and whole grains we include in our diets the better off we'll be. This is not just because they are, generally speaking, low in fat and high in complex nutrients. It's also because even conventionally raised vegetables are tinkered with less than the most "natural" fast or convenience food, and because when you concentrate on vegetables and grains you're more likely to be cooking at home and eating fairly unadulterated food that is within your control.

I do believe that the preparation and consumption of basic good food, especially in the home, improves not only physical health but mental well-being as well. Making satisfying, flavorful meatless meals can easily become a rewarding part of the way you eat and live.

Cooking Basics

Time

There was a time when vegetarian cooking was considered difficult, challenging, and time-consuming. It's true that brown rice takes three times as long to cook as white rice, and that if you're going to eat six-vegetable-stir-fry every night you're going to spend a lot of time peeling and chopping. But "vegetarian" no longer means a complex, constricted way to cook, nor do you have to spend as much time hunting for ingredients for every dish. There are varying levels of difficulty in vegetarian cooking, greater access to ingredients, and, thanks largely to international influences—especially the foods of the Mediterranean and East Asia—there are more vegetarian options, many of which are quick to make.

Time is a precious commodity, no question about it. But you already make a commitment to cook, or at least to eat. Unless you eat in restaurants all the time, you need to put food on the table, no matter what you do. And, as often as not, "convenience" food takes as long to get to the table as real food. Making a bowl of pasta, steaming a vegetable, or preparing a salad are all 20-minute operations, and even preparing all three at once doesn't take more than an hour. And these are dishes in which the ingredients, flavors, and timing are entirely up to you: You know what you are eating and you know what it will taste like. It is a real experience.

The Vegetarian Pantry

You probably already have the makings of several vegetarian meals in your cabinets right now, but if you maintain the right mix of staples you can always be prepared to venture in different directions without so much as a trip to the store.

To stock your pantry and refrigerator, make sure you have on hand:

- pasta and other grains, especially rice
- canned beans, such as cannellini beans, black beans, and chickpeas, and vegetables, especially tomatoes
- canned or boxed vegetable broth
- spices, and dried herbs when fresh are unavailable
- liquid seasonings such as olive oil, vinegar, and soy sauce
- flour, cornmeal, and the like
- nuts and dried fruits
- onions, potatoes, garlic, and other long-keeping vegetables
- UHT (ultra-high temperature-secured), or non-fat dried milk, or soy milk
- eggs and butter (unless you're eating vegan meals)
- tofu (which can be bought in UHT boxes, which keep, unrefrigerated, for months)

With this list alone you will be equipped to make literally dozens of different meals, from pancakes to pasta. When you throw in the fresh ingredients that you're likely to have in the refrigerator as a result of weekly shopping jaunts—vegetables, herbs, fruit, milk, cheese, and other perishables—the result is that you'll be able to prepare many of the recipes in this book without going out to search for special ingredients.

Recipes

All recipes, vegetarian or not, have this in common: They combine a number of ingredients using a given set of techniques. This may seem self-evident, but the choice of ingredients and techniques, along with the clarity of the writing, is what defines a cookbook. I focus on recipes that have broad appeal, and are readily executed even by people who are new to cooking; the techniques I use are classic, but simple and straightforward. I have tried to eliminate all intimidating procedures from this book, and my goal in writing it is probably the same as yours in buying it: To help you make the most of your time in the kitchen, without stress or fuss.

Whenever possible, I have established a basic recipe and used variations to demonstrate a number of different directions in which it can be taken. As you gain in experience and confidence you will begin creating your own variations.

A word about recipe timing. The timing for every recipe is always approximate. The rate at which food cooks is dependent on the moisture content and temperature of the food itself; measurements (which are rarely perfectly accurate); heat level (everyone's "medium-high" heat is not the same, and most ovens are off by at least 25°F in one direction or another); the kind of equipment (some pans conduct heat better than others); even the air temperature. So be sure to use time as a rough guideline, and judge doneness by touch, sight, and taste.

Food Safety

Most food-borne illnesses can be prevented and, because food sickens an estimated six million Americans each year (mostly from salmonella), it's worth taking precautions.

Begin by keeping your hands and all food preparation surfaces and utensils perfectly clean; soap and hot water are good enough, although antibacterial kitchen soaps are probably even better. Wash cutting boards after using (there is no evidence, by the way, that plastic cutting boards are safer than wooden ones), and don't prepare food directly on your counters unless you wash them as well. Change sponges frequently too, and throw your sponges in the washing machine whenever you wash clothes in hot water. Or get into the routine of microwaving your sponge every day: Put it directly in the microwave and blast away until it's too hot to touch. Change your kitchen towel frequently also—at least once a day.

It should go without saying that your refrigerator functions well (35°F is about right, and 40°F is too warm) and that you use it. Food should be stored in the refrigerator until just before cooking (or removed for no more than an hour before cooking if you wish to bring it to room temperature first) or whenever you're not using it. Your freezer should be at 0°F or lower. Thaw foods in the refrigerator, or under cold running water. And never place cooked food on a plate that previously held raw food.

Those are the easy parts of food safety, which everyone should do without question. Cooking foods to their proper degree of doneness is a little trickier, though, generally speaking, it is easier for vegetarians than for meat-eaters. Of common foods, cooked vegetables and grains are by far the safest and the least likely to cause illness (if you're curious, cooked fish comes next, with the most frequent culprits being undercooked poultry and hamburger and, of course, raw shellfish). If you want to be as safe as possible, make sure all food reaches an internal temperature of at least 165°F.

Equipment

Equipment for vegetarian cooking and other cooking are about the same. A good tool to have if you're making a lot of vegetable dishes is a mandoline, a simple slicing device that allows you to make quick work of vegetables; even if your knife skills are good, a mandoline is nice to have, and an inexpensive one costs less than $30. (Be sure to read safety instructions before using.) Also valuable are a good knife, food processor, blender, stockpot, large roasting pan, a grill and grill tools, and an instant-read thermometer.

1 | Sandwiches, Snacks, and Starters

Ⓥ Vegan

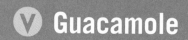

Guacamole

Guacamole—essentially a well-seasoned avocado mash—is among the most delicious dips there is, and among the simplest.

Makes 2 to 4 servings

Time: 10 minutes

1 large or 2 small avocado(s)

1 tablespoon minced onion or shallot

¼ teaspoon minced garlic (optional)

1 teaspoon stemmed, seeded, and minced jalapeño or other fresh chile, or 1 teaspoon chili powder, or to taste

Salt and freshly ground black pepper to taste

1 tablespoon freshly squeezed lime or lemon juice, or to taste

Chopped fresh cilantro leaves for garnish

3 Ways to Vary Guacamole

1 To make guacamole more substantial, add a half cup of peeled, cored, seeded, and diced tomato. Or, use well-drained canned tomatoes, never hard, tasteless ones.

2 Make chunky guacamole by reserving some avocado and chopping it instead of mashing it; then stir it in at the last moment. You can also increase the amount of onion but use mild white or red onion.

3 Replace the chile with some minced chipotle (sold canned, in tomato sauce, as "chipotle in adobo"), for a smoky taste. Or experiment with different chile powders.

1 Cut the avocado(s) in half and reserve the pit(s) if you will not be serving the guacamole right away. Mash the pulp in a bowl with a fork or potato masher, along with the onion or shallot, garlic (if you are using it), chile or chili powder, a little salt and pepper, and 1 tablespoon of lime or lemon juice. Taste and adjust seasoning as necessary.

2 Garnish and serve, or tuck the pit(s) back into the mixture, cover with plastic wrap, and refrigerate for up to 4 hours (this will keep the guacamole from turning brown). Remove the pit(s) before garnishing and serving.

Shopping Tip: You can buy avocados hard, and they will ripen nicely on your kitchen counter. Don't buy them if they're super-mushy or have bruises, and always handle them gently.

Preparation Tips: Cut an avocado in half from pole to pole. If you want to store half, wrap it with the pit intact and refrigerate it that way; this will keep it from turning brown.

Fresh chiles are tricky, because it's hard to predict how hot they'll be. Generally, it's best to remove seeds (the hottest part), and then taste a little piece before deciding how much to add. Wear rubber gloves when working with chiles, or wash your hands very well as soon as you're done handling them.

Hummus

Too often, hummus, which can be used as dip or spread, tastes like nothing but raw garlic; this is milder, made with 1 clove. Of course, you can always add more if you prefer it garlicky. If making the chickpeas from scratch, let them cook a little longer than usual, so that they're nice and soft. Serve this with vegetables, crackers, or pita bread.

Makes at least 8 servings

Time: 20 minutes with precooked chickpeas

2 cups drained well-cooked or canned chickpeas

1/2 cup tahini (sesame paste)

1/4 cup sesame oil from the top of the tahini or olive oil

1 small clove garlic, peeled, or to taste

Salt and freshly ground black pepper to taste

1 tablespoon ground cumin, or to taste, plus a sprinkling for garnish

Juice of 1 lemon, plus more as needed

About 1/3 cup water, or as needed

1 teaspoon olive oil, approximately

3 Ways to Vary Hummus

1 A thinner, "beanier" hummus can be made without any tahini at all. Use more garlic in this case so that the flavor does not become too one-dimensional.

2 Add ground mild chile powder or paprika to taste, or sprinkle some on in place of the cumin.

3 Combine the finished hummus with some mashed roasted eggplant or garnish with roasted red peppers.

1 Place everything except water and 1 teaspoon olive oil in the container of a food processor and begin to process; add water as needed to make a smooth puree.

2 Taste and add more garlic, salt, cumin, or lemon juice as needed. Serve, drizzled with a little olive oil and sprinkled with a bit of cumin.

White Bean Dip Lighter in texture, flavor, and color than hummus. Omit tahini, lemon juice, and water, and use white beans in place of the chickpeas. Combine the beans with 1/4 cup olive oil, the garlic, salt, pepper, 2 teaspoons ground cumin, 1/2 teaspoon ground cinnamon, 1/2 teaspoon ground cardamom, and 1/2 teaspoon ground or peeled and minced fresh ginger. Finish as above.

(V) Bruschetta

Bruschetta is nothing to fuss over: It's simply grilled (or broiled, or even toasted) bread, rubbed with garlic and drizzled with olive oil. There are two requirements: Good coarse, crusty bread and good olive oil. Once you make basic bruschetta, you'll probably want to try variations; I give some, but the possibilities are endless.

Makes 4 appetizer servings

Time: 20 minutes, plus time to preheat the grill

4 slices good bread, preferably cut from a large round loaf

Extra-virgin olive oil

1 clove garlic, halved

Salt to taste

5 Vegetarian Toppings for Bruschetta

Generally, it's best to add toppings when the bruschetta is done to retain its freshness; you shouldn't really cook any of these additions.

1 Chopped fresh herbs

2 Chopped tender greens such as arugula or watercress

3 Small amounts of freshly grated Parmesan, mozzarella, or other cheese

4 Mashed white beans (White Beans, Tuscan Style, page 74, are especially good)

5 Grilled eggplant or zucchini (see Grilled Mixed Vegetables, page 101)

1 Preheat the broiler or grill and adjust the rack so that it is at least 4 inches from the heat source. Brush the bread on one or both sides with a little olive oil and rub one or both sides of each slice with the garlic. (The energy you put into this will determine the intensity of the flavor of the finished product: Rub hard, letting the garlic disintegrate into the bread, and the flavor will be more pronounced; give it a cursory run-through, and the flavor will be mild.) Sprinkle with a little salt.

2 Broil or grill the bread until lightly browned on both sides, taking care not to burn it or toast it all the way through. If you like, drizzle with a little more olive oil and rub with more garlic. Serve immediately.

(V) **Bruschetta with Tomatoes and Basil** Take care not to use overly juicy tomatoes or the bread will become soggy. (For this reason plum tomatoes are best.) Peel, core, seed, and dice 1 small-to-medium tomato per slice of bread. If necessary, drain in a strainer for a few minutes, while you preheat the grill or broiler. Prepare the bread with olive oil and garlic as above and broil or grill 1 side. Turn it over and broil or grill it for 1 minute on the other side, until hot and lightly brown, taking care not to burn. Spread the top with the tomato, then drizzle with olive oil. Garnish with torn or whole basil leaves (or other fresh herb), then drizzle with a little more olive oil and salt if you like.

Gert's Pepper and Onion Sandwich

My mother's favorite sandwich, best with red or yellow peppers, but not bad with green either. She always made this with butter, but extra-virgin olive oil (which barely existed in the United States when I was growing up), is just as good and would make this vegan.

Makes 2 big or 4 small sandwiches

Time: 30 minutes

---

2 tablespoons butter or olive oil, plus more for the rolls if desired

2 bell peppers, preferably red or yellow, stemmed, peeled if desired, seeded, and cut into thin strips

2 medium-to-large onions, cut in half and thinly sliced

Salt and freshly ground black pepper to taste

2 to 4 hard rolls

1 Place the butter or oil in a large, deep skillet over medium heat. When the butter melts or the oil becomes hot, add the peppers and onions. Season with salt and pepper and cook, stirring occasionally, until very tender, about 20 minutes.

2 Butter the rolls if you like. Check the seasoning and pile the pepper-and-onion mixture into the rolls. Serve hot.

Shopping Tip: Yellow and orange peppers seem to be mellowest, but they're usually expensive, so red is the common first choice, green last. Avoid peppers with soft spots or bruises, or those that feel very full—since you buy them by weight, there's no need to pay for lots of seeds. Store peppers, unwrapped, in the vegetable bin, for a week or so.

Preparing Peppers

1	2	3
		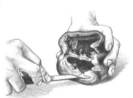

(Step 1) To core a pepper, first cut around the stem. **(Step 2)** Then pull the core out; rinse to remove remaining seeds. **(Step 3)** Alternatively, cut the pepper in half, break out the core, and scrape out the seeds.

Roasted Eggplant Sandwich with Tomato-Garlic Sauce

Ideal on French or Italian bread, this sandwich is also good on a hard roll or any other firm, crusty loaf. Buy the firmest eggplant you can find.

Makes 6 sandwiches

Time: 40 minutes

1 large or 2 medium firm unblemished eggplant, about 1½ pounds total, peeled

3 tablespoons olive oil

1 small onion, minced

Salt and freshly ground black pepper to taste

2 cloves garlic

2 cups drained and chopped canned tomatoes (do not use tomatoes packed in puree)

2 tablespoons minced fresh basil leaves

6 thin slices mozzarella

6 rolls or 2 or 3 loaves of French or Italian bread

1 Preheat the oven to 400°F. Slice the eggplant crosswise into 12 slices, each about ½ inch thick. Brush a baking sheet lightly with 1 tablespoon of olive oil, and place the eggplant slices, in one layer, on the baking sheet. Brush tops of slices with another tablespoon of olive oil. Bake until the eggplant is lightly browned, turn, sprinkle with onion, salt, and pepper, and bake until tender, a total of 20 to 30 minutes.

2 While the eggplant is baking, peel and crush 1 clove of garlic. Place it in a medium skillet with the remaining olive oil and turn the heat to medium. Add the tomatoes and cook briskly over medium heat, stirring frequently, until tomatoes are thick and not at all runny, about 15 minutes. Peel and mince the remaining garlic clove and add it, along with the basil, salt, and pepper, to the tomatoes. Cook an additional 2 minutes over low heat.

3 Use 2 slices of eggplant with a piece of cheese and a dollop of sauce for each sandwich. Serve hot or warm.

Bean Burritos

With cooked beans as the base, you can make great burritos in a flash. Cheese is entirely optional.

Makes 4 servings

Time: 10 minutes with precooked beans

About 2 cups Black Beans with Cumin or Chili (page 77) or canned beans

4 large flour tortillas

1½ to 2 cups grated cheddar, jack, or other semi-hard cheese

2 cups washed, trimmed, dried, and chopped lettuce or other greens

Any spicy sauce or salsa, such as Tomato-Onion Salsa (at right)

Minced cilantro leaves

1 Warm the beans in a small saucepan. To warm the tortillas, wrap them in foil and place in a 300°F oven for about 10 minutes, or stack them between 2 damp paper towels and microwave for 30 to 60 seconds.

2 Spread a portion of cheese onto each tortilla and top with a portion of beans, greens, sauce, and cilantro. Roll up and serve.

Ⓥ Tomato-Onion Salsa

Makes about 1 cup • Time: 10 minutes

This salsa is similar to a finely chopped salad and used as a topping or filling for burritos (or to serve with chips). To use it as a sauce for cold food like leftover vegetables, process until pureed.

1 medium onion, peeled

2 medium tomatoes, cored, peeled, and seeded

1 teaspoon paprika or ¼ to ½ teaspoon cayenne

1 clove garlic, peeled

1 tablespoon any good vinegar, plus more to taste

1 teaspoon salt, or to taste

1 teaspoon sugar

1 tablespoon freshly squeezed lemon or lime juice, or to taste

1 Quarter the onion and tomatoes and whiz them in a food processor or blender with all the other ingredients except the lemon juice. Process just until finely chopped.

2 Taste and add more salt and paprika or cayenne if needed along with the lemon juice or vinegar to taste. Serve or refrigerate for up to a day or two before serving.

3 Simple Additions to Burritos

1 Cooked rice (this is an especially good place to use brown rice)

2 Chopped vegetables, such as bell peppers, mild (white or red) onions, or cucumbers

3 Sour cream or Guacamole (page 2)

Cheese Quesadillas

You can assemble all four quesadillas at once, then wrap and refrigerate them until you're ready to cook. (The cooking itself takes almost no time at all.) If you prefer, dry-sauté these with no oil at all, in a non-stick or well-seasoned cast-iron skillet. As you have no doubt noticed in restaurants, you can add whatever vegetables you want to a quesadilla, but keep the amounts down or you'll wind up with a lumpy, leaking mess.

Makes 8 to 16 servings

Time: 15 minutes

---

4 tablespoons corn or other neutral oil (optional)

8 (8-inch) flour tortillas

1 cup grated cheddar, jack, or other cheese, or a combination (see Shopping Tip)

½ cup minced scallion

¼ cup minced canned green chiles

¼ cup any salsa (optional)

1 The easiest way to make these is to "build" them in the skillet. So: Place 1 tablespoon of oil, if you're using it, in a medium skillet and turn the heat to medium. A minute later, place a tortilla in the skillet. Top with a quarter of the cheese, scallion, chiles, and salsa (if you are using it), then with another tortilla.

2 Cook about 2 minutes, or until the cheese begins to melt. Turn and cook another 2 to 3 minutes, until the cheese is melted and both sides are toasted. Drain if necessary, then cut into wedges and serve, or keep warm until the remaining quesadillas are done.

Shopping Tip: Cheddar and jack cheese are very much alike, and are both best in their sharper (that is, well-aged) forms. If you want authentic taste, the best cheese for quesadillas, and one that is becoming more widely available (especially in cities with a large Hispanic population) is *quesillo* (or queso Oaxaca), which is like mozzarella. This, mixed with cheddar or the similar *queso chilmalma*, makes for the ideal quesadilla.

Basic Frittata

The basic frittata is very much like the basic omelet, but even easier to master.

Makes 4 servings

Time: About 30 minutes

2 tablespoons butter or olive oil

5 or 6 eggs

½ cup freshly grated Parmesan or other cheese

Salt and freshly ground black pepper to taste

Minced fresh parsley leaves for garnish

1 Preheat the oven to 350°F.

2 Place the butter or oil in a medium-to-large ovenproof skillet, preferably non-stick, and turn the heat to medium. While it's heating, beat together the eggs, cheese, salt, and pepper. When the butter melts or the oil is hot, pour the eggs into the skillet and turn the heat to medium-low. Cook, undisturbed, for about 10 minutes, or until the bottom of the frittata is firm.

3 Transfer the skillet to the oven. Bake, checking every 5 minutes or so, just until the top of the frittata is no longer runny, 10 to 20 minutes more. (To speed things up, turn on the broiler, but be very careful not to overcook.) Garnish and serve hot or at room temperature.

Herb Frittata Mince about 1 cup of fresh herbs—chervil, parsley, dill, or basil should make up the bulk of them, but others such as tarragon, oregano, marjoram, or chives may be added in smaller quantities—and stir them into the egg mixture just before turning it into the skillet. Proceed as above, garnishing with whatever fresh herb you like.

5 Vegetarian Additions to Frittate

Almost anything you find appetizing can be used in a frittata; the basic proportions are 1 to 2 cups filling for every 4 or 5 eggs. These may be used alone or in combination:

1 Peeled, seeded, and diced tomato

2 Sautéed mushrooms

3 Sautéed potatoes and onions

4 Sautéed onion, fresh tomato, and basil

5 Chopped, steamed spinach or chard, mixed with a dash of lemon and nutmeg or sautéed, with minced garlic, in olive oil

Pot Stickers or Steamed Dumplings

Make these wrapped snacks with round wonton wrappers, about 3 or 4 inches in diameter. They can be cooked as sautéed pot stickers or steamed dumplings.

Makes at least 24 dumplings,
enough for 4 to 8 people

Time: 30 to 45 minutes

½ cup finely minced scallion, both white
and green parts, or chives

½ cup chopped fresh shiitake mushrooms,
caps only (save the stems for stock)

¼ cup minced bamboo shoots, water
chestnuts, cabbage, or peeled and
shredded carrots

1 teaspoon minced garlic

1 teaspoon peeled and minced or grated
fresh ginger

Salt and freshly ground black pepper
to taste

1 tablespoon soy sauce

½ teaspoon sugar

1 teaspoon dark sesame oil

24 or more round wonton wrappers

4 tablespoons peanut oil, if pan-cooking

¾ cup water, plus a little more

1 Combine the first nine ingredients. Place 1 rounded teaspoon of filling on each wonton wrapper, then fold the wrapper over to form a semicircle (see illustrations on page 11). Seal with a few drops of water. Keep the finished dumplings under a moist towel while you work.

2 To make pot stickers, put the peanut oil in a large, deep skillet and turn the heat to medium-high. Place the dumplings, 1 at a time, into the skillet, seam side up. Do not crowd; cook in 2 batches if necessary. Cover the pot and cook for about 5 minutes. Uncover and add ¾ cup water to the pot; re-cover and cook another 2 minutes, then uncover and cook about 3 minutes more, or until water has evaporated. Remove the dumplings with a spatula and serve with dipping sauce.

3 To steam the dumplings, set up a steamer; to improvise, fit a heatproof plate or a rack above 1 inch or so of boiling water in a covered pot. Steam the dumplings in 1 or 2 batches, for about 10 minutes per batch. Serve hot, with dipping sauce.

Shopping Tip: Supermarkets usually stock both square and round wonton wrappers; either can be frozen for later use. Square wrappers are a little easier to handle, but round ones yield a less doughy dumpling; the choice is yours.

Ⓥ Soy and Sesame Dipping Sauce

Makes about ½ cup • Time: 10 minutes

A basic recipe that is almost infinitely variable. This and the variation also make terrific marinades.

1 tablespoon sesame seeds, toasted

¼ cup soy sauce

1 tablespoon dark sesame oil

1½ teaspoons rice or other light vinegar

½ teaspoon minced garlic

1 tablespoon peeled and minced fresh ginger or 1 teaspoon ground ginger

½ teaspoon sugar

Combine all the ingredients and stir briefly to blend. Taste; if the mixture is too strongly flavored (which it may be, if your soy sauce is strong), add water, a teaspoon at a time, until the flavor mellows. Use within 1 hour.

Ⓥ **Fiery Peanut Sauce** Omit sesame seeds and oil. Add 2 tablespoons finely chopped peanuts and 1 tablespoon stemmed, seeded, and minced fresh hot chiles, such as pequíns or jalapeños. Taste and add more chiles if you like.

Making Pot Stickers

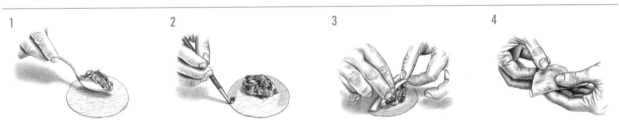

1   2   3   4

(**Step 1**) Place a teaspoon of filling on ¹/₂ of the dough. (**Step 2**) Brush circumference of the circle with a little water or beaten egg. (**Steps 3–4**) Fold over and pinch tightly to seal.

2 | Salads

Ⓥ Vegan

Carrot Salad with Cumin

Here's a simple salad in a typically North African style, one that can add both flavor and surprise to any meal. It features carrots, complemented by the sweetness of fresh oranges and the distinctive earthiness of ground cumin.

Makes 4 servings

Time: 15 minutes

1½ pounds carrots, peeled and grated

Juice of 2 oranges

Juice of 1 lemon

2 tablespoons extra-virgin olive oil

Salt and freshly ground black pepper to taste

1 teaspoon ground cumin, or more to taste

1 Use the julienne cutter of a food processor or a hand grater to cut the carrots into fine shreds, or cut into ⅛-inch-thick slices with a knife.

2 Blend the remaining ingredients and pour the dressing over the carrots. Toss and serve.

Root Vegetables with Cumin This salad is equally good with grated celeriac, jicama, or sunchokes, for some (or even all) of the carrots, using the same dressing. Celeriac, a knobby, rough textured root, is closely related to celery and tastes like it; trim the exterior portions with a paring knife before using. Jicama is easier to peel, its flesh being somewhat smoother, but is also a large root. Sunchokes, also called Jerusalem artichokes, are neither from Jerusalem nor artichokes, but they're small, good tasting roots that come from a form of sunflower; peel before using.

Tomato, Mozzarella, and Basil Salad

This is barely more than the three ingredients listed above, so all three must be of excellent quality. I like to salt the tomatoes a little bit before assembling the salad—it removes some of their excess liquid—but it isn't strictly necessary.

Makes 4 servings

Time: 5 to 15 minutes

4 medium perfectly ripe tomatoes

Salt to taste

8 (¼-inch-thick) slices fresh mozzarella, plus more if desired

8 basil leaves, washed and dried

Freshly ground black pepper to taste

Extra-virgin olive oil for drizzling

1   Core and cut the tomatoes into about ½-inch-thick slices (page 41). If you like, lay them on a board and sprinkle them lightly with salt. Set the board at an angle so the liquid can drain into the sink (or a bowl; it makes a refreshing drink).

2   Layer tomatoes, mozzarella, and basil on a platter or 4 individual plates. Sprinkle with salt and pepper, drizzle with olive oil, and serve.

Classic American Potato Salad

Low-starch, or waxy, potatoes are best for salad (and for all other boiling purposes). These are typically called "new" potatoes—young potatoes are always lower in starch—and may be red or white. Yukon gold potatoes, which have a medium starch content, will do the job as well. Just steer clear of russet, Idaho, or other "baking" potatoes.

Makes 4 servings

Time: 30 minutes, plus cooling time

1½ pounds waxy potatoes, such as red new potatoes

½ cup minced fresh parsley leaves

¼ cup minced onion

Mayonnaise to taste (start with ½ cup)

Salt and freshly ground black pepper to taste

1 Bring a medium pot of water to a boil; salt it. Peel the potatoes if you like (or wash and scrub them well), then cut them into bite-sized pieces; cook them in the water until tender but still firm and not at all mushy, 15 minutes or so. Drain, rinse in cold water for a minute, then drain again.

2 Toss the still-warm potatoes with the parsley and onion. Add mayonnaise until the mixture is as creamy as you like. Season with salt and pepper and refrigerate until ready to serve. (You may prepare the salad in advance up to this point; cover and refrigerate for up to a day, then bring to room temperature before serving.)

V Potato Salad with Mustard While they're still warm, combine the cooked, peeled, and cut-up potatoes with parsley, onion (or shallot, which is even better), and whole-grain mustard, thinned with a little white wine or mild vinegar (like rice vinegar) to taste.

4 Vegetarian Additions to Potato Salad

1 Minced red pepper, fresh or roasted (or use canned pimentos)

2 Minced fresh herbs to taste

3 Cooked fresh peas

4 Minced pickle, preferably sweet pickle

Ⓥ Spicy Coleslaw

More interesting, more flavorful, and far less fat-laden than traditional coleslaw, but if the creamy version is your preference, see the variation.

Makes about 2 quarts

Time: 20 minutes

2 tablespoons Dijon mustard

2 tablespoons sherry or balsamic vinegar

1/2 cup olive, peanut, or vegetable oil

1 tablespoon sugar

6 cups cored and shredded napa, savoy, green, and/or red cabbage

2 red bell peppers, stemmed, peeled if desired, seeded, and diced

1 cup diced scallions

Salt and freshly ground black pepper to taste

1/4 cup minced fresh parsley leaves

1 Whisk together the mustard and vinegar in a small bowl; add the oil a little at a time, whisking all the while.

2 Add sugar and whisk to dissolve.

3 Combine the cabbage, peppers, and scallions, and toss with the dressing. Season with salt and pepper and refrigerate until ready to serve (it's best to let this rest for an hour or so before serving to allow the flavors to mellow; you can let it sit longer, up to 24 hours, if you like). Just before serving, toss with parsley.

Shopping Tip: Cabbage is a year-round vegetable, widely shipped and found locally when the weather is cool. Reject any cabbages with yellow, soft, or loose leaves.

Preparation Tips: All head cabbage, regardless of color, as well as napa cabbage, should be cored before shredding or cooking. First remove a couple of layers of the outer leaves. Then use a thin-bladed knife to cut a cone-shaped section out of the core, making the wide end of the cone a circle about 1/2 inch wider than the core itself.

To shred head cabbage, just cut the cabbage into quarters (or eighths, if it is large), and cross-cut thinly; it will shred itself. To shred napa cabbage, just cross-cut; no quartering is necessary.

Mayo Coleslaw To make the more traditional style of coleslaw, omit the oil and vinegar and combine the other ingredients with about 1/2 cup of mayonnaise thinned with a tablespoon or 2 of milk. The mustard is optional (as are the peppers and scallions) and, typically, more sugar is added.

Beet and Fennel Salad

This is a dish of lovely contrasts and syntheses: red and white, with the slight licorice flavor of tarragon playing with the crunchy fennel and the smooth beets.

Makes 4 to 6 servings

Time: 1 to 1½ hours

4 medium beets, a little more than 1 pound

1 fennel bulb

2 tablespoons extra-virgin olive oil

1 tablespoon freshly squeezed lemon juice

1 tablespoon minced fresh basil leaves, 1 teaspoon minced fresh tarragon leaves, or ½ teaspoon dried tarragon, plus additional chopped fresh herb for garnish (optional)

Salt and freshly ground black pepper to taste

1. Preheat the oven to 400°F. Wash the beets well. Wrap them individually in foil and place them on a baking sheet or roasting pan.

2. Cook, undisturbed, for 45 to 90 minutes, until a thin-bladed knife pierces one with little resistance (they may cook at different rates; remove each one when it is done). While they're cooking, trim the fennel and chop it into ½- to 1-inch dice.

3. Remove the beets and plunge them into ice water until cool. Peel them and cut them into pieces the same size as the fennel.

4. Toss the beets, fennel, and the remaining ingredients together and serve immediately. If you plan to let the salad sit, hold out the lemon juice until the last minute (and don't be surprised when the fennel turns red). Garnish, if you like, with a bit of chopped fresh herb.

Shopping Tip: With fennel (also called anise), you're primarily interested in the bulb, not the stalks. It should be tight and greenish white, with little or no browning or shriveled parts. Store fennel, loosely wrapped, in the vegetable bin, for up to a week—but use it as soon as you can.

Preparation Tip: Trim fennel's feathery fronds and hollow stalks; use them for seasoning or discard. Trim off the hard bottom and cut vertical slices through the bulb. Or cut in half, dig out the core, and cut into thin strips to then dice for salads, as in this recipe, or for sautéing, braising, or roasting (but not grilling, where you need larger pieces).

Pear and Gorgonzola Salad

Something about this combination is magical: the smooth sweetness of the pears, the creamy saltiness of the cheese, the crunchiness of walnuts . . . it's a great salad.

Makes 4 servings

Time: 20 minutes

1 cup walnut halves

4 to 6 cups torn mixed salad greens (trimmed, washed, and dried)

½ cup Vinaigrette (at right)

2 pears, peeled, cored, and cut into slices

¼ pound Gorgonzola, Roquefort, or other good creamy blue cheese

1 Place the walnuts in a dry skillet and turn the heat to medium. Toast, shaking the pan frequently, until they are aromatic and beginning to darken in color, 3 to 5 minutes. Set aside to cool while you prepare the other ingredients.

2 Toss the greens with most of the vinaigrette and divide among 4 plates. Decorate with pear slices and crumble the cheese over all. Crumble or coarsely chop the walnuts and scatter them over the salad. Drizzle with the remaining vinaigrette and serve.

Shopping Tip: Good blue cheese should be quite soft, though not runny. It can be made from the milk of cows, sheep, or goats. The best known blue sheep cheese is Roquefort. Usually, however, it's easier to find a good Gorgonzola or Stilton (both made from cow's milk), or a good domestic variety, like Maytag blue.

Ⓥ Vinaigrette

Makes 1 cup • Time: 5 minutes

Emulsified—or thoroughly blended—vinaigrettes are only important if you care. I often just toss everything in a bowl and whisk it for 30 seconds or so.

¼ cup good vinegar, such as sherry, balsamic, or high-quality red or white wine, plus more to taste

½ teaspoon salt, plus more if needed

½ teaspoon Dijon mustard (optional)

¾ cup extra-virgin olive oil, plus more if needed

2 teaspoons minced shallots (optional)

Freshly ground black pepper to taste

1 Briefly mix the vinegar, salt, and optional mustard with an immersion blender, food processor, or blender, or with a fork or wire whisk.

2 Slowly add the oil in a stream (drop by drop if whisking) until an emulsion forms; or just whisk everything together briefly. Add the remaining oil faster, but still in a stream.

3 Taste to adjust salt and add more oil or vinegar if needed. Add the shallots and pepper. This is best made fresh but will keep, refrigerated, for a few days; bring back to room temperature before using.

Chickpeas with Lemon

This chickpea salad is great to have around. Eat it warm, at room temperature, or cold—but add the lemon juice at the last minute for maximum flavor.

Makes 6 to 8 servings

Time: About 2 hours for dried chickpeas, 15 minutes for pre-cooked

---

2 cups dried chickpeas, washed and picked over (see Bean Tips, page 73) or about 4 cups cooked or canned chickpeas

1 bay leaf

1 clove garlic, peeled

2 tablespoons minced shallot, onion, or scallion

3 tablespoons extra-virgin olive oil

Salt and freshly ground black pepper to taste

Freshly squeezed lemon juice to taste

Minced fresh parsley or cilantro leaves for garnish

1   If you're using dried chickpeas, cook them, with the bay leaf and garlic, according to the recipe for Basic Beans (page 72), until they are quite tender. If you're using canned beans, warm them for a few minutes with the bay leaf and garlic. Remove the bay leaf and garlic and drain.

2   While the chickpeas are still warm, toss them with the shallot and olive oil and season with salt and pepper. (You may prepare the salad in advance up to this point; cover and refrigerate for up to a day, then bring to room temperature before proceeding.) Serve warm or at room temperature; just before serving add plenty of lemon juice and garnish.

Ⓥ White Bean Salad

A simple and satisfying salad. For speed, make it with canned white beans, but if you have the time, home-cooked beans are preferable.

Makes 4 servings

Time: 15 minutes to 2 hours

1½ cups dried white beans, washed and picked over (see Bean Tips, page 73), or 3 cups cooked or canned white beans, drained

1 teaspoon fresh thyme, marjoram, or sage leaves or ½ teaspoon dried herb

3 shallots or scallions, minced

¼ cup minced red bell pepper

6 tablespoons olive oil, approximately

About 2 tablespoons balsamic, sherry, or wine vinegar

½ teaspoon Dijon mustard

Salt and freshly ground black pepper to taste

1   If you're using dried beans, cook them according to the recipe for Basic Beans (page 72), until they are quite tender. Drain them and place them (or the canned beans) in a medium saucepan with half of the thyme; turn the heat to medium and cook for 5 minutes, or until just heated through. Turn off the heat, add the shallots or scallions and red pepper, and cool.

2   Place the olive oil, vinegar, remaining thyme, and mustard in a jar with a lid and shake well; or use a small food processor, blender, or immersion blender. Taste for seasoning and add salt, pepper, and additional oil or vinegar as desired. Pour over the beans and, if you have time, let rest for an hour (or up to 24 hours, refrigerated) before serving.

3 Simple Ideas For White Beans

Cooked white beans freeze well (freeze them in their liquid, in a covered container) and are a good addition to any salad. You might also try these ideas.

1 Make White Bean Dip, page 3.

2 Combine warm white beans with the best extra-virgin olive oil you can find, a little bit of minced garlic, and a lot of salt and pepper.

3 Add cooked white beans to any stew or soup.

Panzanella (Bread Salad)

One classic Italian way to use stale bread is to toast it for extra flavor, soften it with liquid, and use it as the backbone of panzanella, a classic Italian bread salad. If you like, add capers and/or minced roasted red pepper to the mix. Without those additions, this recipe is basic, but remains a delicious midsummer treat.

Makes 4 servings

Time: 30 minutes

4 medium perfectly ripe tomatoes, cored and peeled (page 41)

About 1/2 teaspoon salt, plus more if needed

1 clove garlic, peeled

8 thick slices good bread, preferably a couple of days old

1 teaspoon fresh oregano, marjoram, or thyme leaves or 1/4 cup minced fresh basil or parsley leaves

1/3 cup extra-virgin olive oil

1 tablespoon balsamic or other good vinegar, or to taste

Freshly ground black pepper to taste

1 Use your fingers to remove the liquid center and seeds from the tomatoes; place in a strainer over a bowl and add the meat of the tomatoes. Sprinkle the tomatoes with about 1/2 teaspoon of salt and set aside while you prepare the bread.

2 Preheat the broiler. Cut the garlic clove in half and rub the bread all over with it. Toast the bread under the broiler, taking care not to burn it. When it is nicely browned and crisp throughout, cool it for a minute, then tear it into bite-sized pieces. Place it in a bowl with the juices extracted from the tomatoes.

3 Discard the tomato seeds and chop the meat into smaller pieces. When the bread has softened a bit, add the tomatoes, herb, oil, vinegar, and some black pepper. Taste and adjust seasoning as necessary; serve immediately.

Ⓥ Tabbouleh

Bulgur (or bulghur), a traditional grain of the Middle East, is wheat which is first steamed, then hulled, dried, then cracked. The result is a quick-cooking grain (in fact, you don't even cook some bulgur, you just soak it) that filled the historical need of conserving fuel and today provides convenience and great flavor.

The Americanized version of this dish focuses on cracked wheat and tomato, but this more authentic Middle Eastern dish is little more than loads of herbs given substance. It's delicious.

Makes 4 to 6 servings

Time: About 40 minutes

½ cup fine-grind (Number 1) or medium-grind (Number 2) bulgur

2 cups minced fresh parsley leaves

1 cup minced fresh mint leaves

2 cups cored, seeded, and chopped tomatoes (page 41)

1 small red or white onion, finely chopped

½ cup extra-virgin olive oil

4 tablespoons freshly squeezed lemon juice, or to taste

Salt and freshly ground black pepper to taste

1 Soak the bulgur in water to cover until tender, 15 to 30 minutes. Drain well, squeezing out as much of the water as possible.

2 Combine the bulgur with the parsley, mint, tomatoes, and onion; whisk together the olive oil and lemon juice and toss with the salad. Season with salt and pepper and taste; adjust seasoning if necessary. You can refrigerate this for a few hours if you like, but let it warm up a bit before serving.

Shopping Tip: Bulgur comes in 4 grinds: *Fine* (Number 1) is almost always just soaked rather than cooked. *Medium* (Number 2) can be soaked or cooked. *Coarse* (Number 3) must be cooked. *Very coarse* (Number 4) you won't see often. Most supermarkets stock medium, which you can consider all-purpose. Fine-grind and coarse can be found in many natural foods stores, specialty food markets, and Middle Eastern stores.

3 | Soups

Ⓥ Vegan

"Boiled Water"

This is a simple traditional peasant soup that needs no stock, yet is garlicky, quite delicious, and satisfying.

Makes 4 servings

Time: 20 minutes

4 cups water

6 to 10 cloves garlic, lightly crushed

1 bay leaf

Salt and freshly ground black pepper
to taste

¼ cup extra-virgin olive oil

4 thick slices French or Italian bread
(slightly stale bread is fine)

½ cup freshly grated Parmesan
or Pecorino Romano cheese

Minced fresh parsley leaves for garnish

1 Combine the first 4 ingredients in a saucepan or stockpot and bring to a boil. Cover partially and turn the heat to very low. Simmer gently for 15 minutes.

2 While the soup is cooking, place the olive oil in a large skillet over medium heat. Brown the slices of bread in the oil, turning occasionally, for a total of about 5 minutes.

3 Put the bread in bowls and top with the grated cheese. Strain the soup into the bowls, garnish, and serve.

Garlic Soup with Egg About 4 minutes before you want to serve, carefully break 4 eggs into the simmering soup. Cook, occasionally spooning some of the liquid over the tops of the eggs. When they're set, spoon each onto a piece of the toasted bread—already in bowls—and top with the liquid. Or, for extra thick (and protein-rich) soup, break an egg or two into the liquid and stir, just before serving.

Mushroom-Barley Soup

This is a quick, super-hearty soup that is made without stock; with a loaf of bread, it makes a fine weeknight meal.

Makes at least 6 servings

Time: About 1 hour

---

8 cups water

½ cup pearled barley

½ cup peeled and roughly chopped carrots

½ cup peeled and roughly chopped onion

½ cup peeled and roughly chopped celery

½ ounce dried porcini mushrooms

½ pound fresh mushrooms, any kind

Salt and freshly ground black pepper to taste

½ cup snipped fresh dill, minced chives, or minced parsley leaves

1   Put the water in a stockpot and bring to a boil. Add the barley, carrots, onion, and celery.

2   Turn the heat to low and partially cover; the mixture should be bubbling, but only a little. Soak the dried mushrooms in warm water to cover until tender (about 10 minutes), and clean, trim, and slice the fresh mushrooms.

3   Strain the soaked mushrooms; reserve their liquid. Add all the mushrooms to the simmering soup. Add the mushroom-soaking liquid to the soup. Simmer the soup for 30 to 45 minutes more, until the barley and vegetables are tender.

4   Taste and season with salt and pepper. Stir in half the dill, chives, or parsley, then top individual servings with the remaining herb.

Shopping Tip: Almost all barley is pearled—its hard outer husk is removed—but whole barley is sold in many health food stores. Be sure you know what you're getting; whole barley takes a couple of hours to cook, and never becomes completely tender.

Kale and Potato Soup

Kale soup, a Portuguese specialty, is frequently spiced with sausage or thickened with cream. Here, however, its assertive flavor is complemented by marjoram, and pureed potato adds a pleasant texture without fat or meat. Substitute collard greens for the kale, if you like.

Makes 4 servings

Time: 30 minutes

1 large baking potato, cut into eighths

1 clove garlic, lightly smashed

5 cups Vegetable Stock (at right), store-bought vegetable broth, or water, preferably warmed

About 3 cups roughly chopped kale leaves (stripped from the stalks and well rinsed before chopping)

1 teaspoon fresh marjoram or oregano leaves or 1/2 teaspoon dried marjoram or oregano

1 bay leaf

Salt and freshly ground black pepper to taste

1 Combine the potato, garlic, and 2 cups of the stock or water in a medium saucepan and turn the heat to medium-high. Cook until the potato is soft, about 15 minutes; cool slightly. (You may prepare the soup in advance up to this point. Cover, refrigerate for up to 2 days, and reheat before proceeding.)

2 At the same time, cook the kale in the remaining stock or water with the marjoram and bay leaf until tender, about 10 minutes. Remove the bay leaf.

3 Puree the potato, garlic, and stock or water together; the mixture will be thick. Stir it into the simmering kale, season with salt and pepper, and heat through. Serve immediately.

Shopping Tip: Kale, like collards—its close, non-crinkly relative—has large, dark green, almost leathery leaves. But both greens (and they are interchangeable) are at their sweetest when grown in cool weather.

Cooking Tip: There's only one trick to cooking collards and kale: Make sure you cook them long enough to soften the stems. Undercooked stems are unpleasantly tough and chewy. (One sure way to prevent this is to avoid collards with stems more than 1/8 inch thick.)

V Vegetable Stock

Makes 3 quarts • Time: About 1½ hours, largely unattended

There is really only one rule I slavishly follow when making vegetable stock, and it is to roast the vegetables before simmering them. The browning adds body and flavor that you don't get otherwise. Aside from that, you can substitute freely among these vegetables. Only leeks or onions, carrots, and celery are truly essential.

2 well-washed leeks, cut in half, or 2 large onions, quartered (don't bother to peel them)

4 carrots, peeled and cut in half

2 celery stalks, cut in half

2 parsnips, peeled and cut in half (optional)

2 white turnips, peeled and quartered (optional)

2 potatoes, peeled or well washed and quartered (optional; use these if you don't use the parsnips or turnips)

6 cloves garlic or 3 shallots, unpeeled

1 cup fresh mushrooms, trimmed, or mushroom stems, or ¼ cup reconstituted dried mushrooms with their soaking liquid

4 tablespoons extra-virgin olive oil

10 sprigs fresh parsley

2 or 3 sprigs fresh thyme

10 peppercorns

½ cup white wine

Salt to taste

2 quarts water (8 cups), plus 4 cups water

1   Preheat the oven to 400°F. Place the leeks, carrots, celery, parsnips, turnips, potatoes, garlic, and fresh mushrooms (hold off on adding reconstituted dried mushrooms) in a large roasting pan and drizzle with the olive oil; put the pan in the oven.

2   Roast, shaking the pan occasionally and turning the ingredients once or twice, until everything is nicely browned. This will take about 45 minutes; don't rush it.

3   Use a slotted spoon to scoop all the ingredients into a stockpot; add the remaining ingredients and the 2 quarts of water. Turn the heat to high.

4   Place the roasting pan over a burner set to high and add 2 to 4 cups of water, depending on the depth of the pan. Bring it to a boil and cook, scraping off all the bits of food that have stuck to the bottom. Pour this mixture into the stockpot (along with 2 more cups of water if you only used 2 cups for deglazing).

5   Bring the contents of the stockpot just about to a boil, then partially cover and adjust the heat so the mixture sends up a few bubbles at a time. Cook until the vegetables are very soft, 30 to 45 minutes.

6   Strain, pressing on the vegetables to extract as much juice as possible. Taste and add salt if necessary. Refrigerate, then skim any hardened fat from the surface if you like. Refrigerate for 4 to 5 days or freeze.

Tomato Soup, Three Ways

Make this with fresh tomatoes in late summer. The rest of the year, use good canned tomatoes.

Makes 4 servings

Time: 30 minutes

2 tablespoons extra-virgin olive oil or butter

1 large onion, sliced

1 carrot, peeled and diced

Salt and freshly ground black pepper to taste

3 cups cored, peeled, seeded, and chopped tomatoes (canned are fine; include their juice)

1 teaspoon fresh thyme leaves or ½ teaspoon dried thyme or 1 tablespoon minced fresh basil leaves

2 to 3 cups vegetable stock, preferably warmed

Minced fresh parsley or basil leaves for garnish

1 Place the oil or butter in a large, deep saucepan or casserole and turn the heat to medium. A minute later, add the onion and carrot. Season with salt and pepper and cook, stirring, until the onion begins to soften, about 5 minutes.

2 Add the tomatoes and the herb and cook until the tomatoes break up, about 10 minutes. Add 2 cups of stock. (You may prepare the soup in advance up to this point. Cover, refrigerate for up to 2 days, and reheat before proceeding.) Adjust seasoning; if the mixture is too thick, add a little stock or water. Garnish and serve.

Ⓥ **Pureed Tomato Soup** Increase the tomatoes to 4 cups and reduce the stock to 1 cup. When the soup is done, puree it carefully in a blender or pass it through a food mill. Reheat, garnish, and serve, preferably with Baked Croutons (page 37).

Cream of Tomato Soup In the above variation, substitute 1 cup cream or half-and-half for the stock, added just before pureeing.

Cream of Broccoli (or Any Vegetable) Soup

There are thousands of recipes for true cream of vegetable soups, but the differences among them are subtle at best. Basically, you cook the vegetable you want with good flavorings until it's done. Then you puree it and reheat it with cream. (The addition of rice or potatoes makes the soup smooth and creamy without outrageous amounts of cream. One-quarter cup is enough to lighten the color and smooth the texture; 1 full cup lends an incomparable richness.) You can also replace the cream with milk or yogurt. Try varying the seasonings too, adding whatever fresh herbs and spices appeal to you.

Makes 4 servings

Time: 30 minutes

About 1 pound broccoli, trimmed and cut up, to yield about 4 loosely packed cups broccoli, or the equivalent amount of cauliflower, carrots, turnips, celery, or other vegetable

1/2 cup rice or 1 medium baking potato, peeled and cut into quarters

4 cups Vegetable Stock (page 29), store-bought vegetable broth, or water

Salt and freshly ground black pepper to taste

1/4 to 1 cup heavy or light cream or half-and-half

Minced fresh parsley leaves or chives for garnish

1 Combine the broccoli, rice or potato, and stock or water in a large, deep saucepan or casserole and turn the heat to medium-high. Bring to a boil, then lower the heat to medium and cook until the vegetables are very tender, about 15 minutes.

2 Cool slightly, then puree in the pot with an immersion blender or in a food mill or in a blender. (You may prepare the soup in advance up to this point. Cover, refrigerate for up to 2 days, and reheat before proceeding.)

3 Return to the pot and reheat over medium-low heat. Add salt and pepper, then add the cream; heat through again, garnish, and serve.

Preparation Tips: To prepare broccoli, strip the stalk of leaves, if any (these can be cooked along with the tops and eaten, if you like). Remove the bottom inch of the stalk, or wherever it has dried out. Peel the tough outer skin of the broccoli stalk with a paring knife or vegetable peeler. (To peel with a paring knife, hold the broccoli upside down; grasp a bit of the skin right at the bottom, between the paring knife and your thumb. Pull down to remove a strip of the skin.) If you like, cut the stalk into equal-length pieces and break the head into florets.

An immersion blender is basically a stick with a blender blade on the end of it. It was created to puree large quantities of soups in restaurants while they remained in the pot. Models designed for home use are not nearly as powerful as regular blenders, but they make creaming soups less labor intensive and messy than using a standard blender.

Creamy Pumpkin or Winter Squash Soup

This soup requires only a few ingredients, one of which is water, and bread as a thickener. It's fast and delicious.

Makes 4 servings

Time: 45 minutes

2 pounds pumpkin or winter squash, peeled, seeded, and cut into 1- to 2-inch cubes

6 cloves garlic, peeled

4 cups water

4 or 5 slices stale, crustless French or Italian bread

Salt and freshly ground black pepper to taste

Minced fresh parsley leaves for garnish

1 Combine the pumpkin and garlic in a large pot, along with the water (if you use stock the flavor will be better, but it is far from essential), and turn the heat to medium-high.

2 Bring to a boil, then turn the heat to medium-low and cook for about 30 minutes, until the pumpkin is very soft. (You may prepare the soup in advance up to this point. Cover, refrigerate for up to 2 days, and reheat before proceeding.)

3 Tear the bread into pieces and add them to the broth; cook 5 more minutes.

4 Puree the soup in a food mill or blender, reheat, and add salt and pepper. Garnish and serve.

Shopping Tip: Winter squash gets sweeter later in the season; November and December's squashes are more delicious than those from early fall. Though the flesh of all of them is roughly equivalent, I buy butternut squash because it's easiest to peel—use a paring knife, and don't worry too much about precision.

Cooking Tip: You can make this soup without the garlic, or the bread. In fact, combining squash with water or stock and seasonings, then pureeing, produces a soup that is so creamy it's hard to believe it has no dairy. For extra thickness, you can stir in some milk, cream, sour cream, or yogurt. Another good addition is roasted (or boiled) and chopped chestnuts, or sliced and quickly browned apples.

V Fiery Pumpkin Seeds

Makes 2 cups • Time: About 45 minutes

If you're cleaning out a pumpkin or squash anyway, make the most of the seeds. (Or just substitute store-bought pumpkin seeds, also called *pepitas,* to make this great snack.)

Crisp-baked pumpkin seeds are fine with salt, but adding some fire turns them into a great pre-dinner tidbit, or a fine snack with beer. You can also make this with any spice mix, such as curry powder or chili powder.

2 cups (approximately) fresh pumpkin seeds

2 tablespoons light vegetable or olive oil

About 1 teaspoon salt

About 1 teaspoon cayenne, or more if you like

1/2 teaspoon cumin, optional

1 Separate the seeds from the pumpkin strings by rinsing them in a bowl full of water. Dry the seeds between paper towels.

2 Mix the oil with salt, cayenne, and cumin, and toss the seeds with this mixture until they are coated. (Then wash your hands well.)

3 Bake the seeds on a baking sheet in a 350°F oven for 30 to 45 minutes, tossing occasionally, until they are tan and crisp, or spread the seeds between 2 layers of paper towels and microwave on high for 10 to 15 minutes, stirring every 5 minutes, until seeds are tan and crisp. They will crisp up further as they cool.

Ⓥ Lentil Soup

Though lentil soup is often made with meat, to me the key ingredients are the lentils and the carrots—something about their sweetness really makes the thing work. Of course I wouldn't cook the soup without garlic, either.

Makes 4 servings

Time: About 45 minutes

1 cup lentils, washed and picked over

1 bay leaf

Several sprigs fresh thyme
or few pinches dried thyme

1 carrot, peeled and cut into ½-inch
or smaller cubes

1 celery stalk, cut into ½-inch
or smaller cubes

About 6 cups water, Vegetable Stock
(page 29), or store-bought vegetable
broth, preferably warmed

2 tablespoons olive oil

1 onion, chopped

1 teaspoon minced garlic

Salt and freshly ground black pepper
to taste

1   Place the lentils, bay leaf, thyme, carrot, and celery in a medium pot with 6 cups of the water or stock. Bring to a boil, then turn the heat to low and cook, stirring occasionally.

2   Meanwhile, place the olive oil in a small skillet and turn the heat to medium-low. Add the onion and cook, stirring, until it softens. Add the garlic and stir. Cook for 1 minute more.

3   When the lentils are tender—they usually take about 30 minutes—fish out the bay leaf and the thyme sprigs and pour the onion mixture into the soup. (You may prepare the soup in advance up to this point. Cover, refrigerate for up to 2 days, and reheat before proceeding.)

4   Add more water or stock if necessary; the mixture should be thick, but still quite soupy. Season with salt and pepper and serve.

Shopping Tip: Ordinary lentils may be greenish brown or brownish green, but the best are dark green, and are originally from France. Called *lentilles de Puy,* they're smaller than most, and they remain firm throughout cooking, never becoming quite as mushy as the others.

Cooking Tip: When using lentils in soup, it's best to remove about half of them, puree them, and then return them to the pot, giving you a wonderful texture of half puree, half firm lentils.

Ⓥ **Spicy Vegetarian Lentil Soup** Omit the bay leaf. In Step 2, cook the onion and garlic as above, then add 1 cup chopped tomatoes (canned are fine; add their liquid to the simmering lentils); ½ cup minced fresh parsley or cilantro leaves; 1 tablespoon peeled and minced fresh ginger; ¼ teaspoon cayenne, or to taste; and ½ teaspoon ground cumin. Stir, then proceed as above.

Pasta and Bean Soup

A warm, delicious classic known as *Pasta e Fagioli* (or colloquially as Pasta "Fazool"), which can be varied in many ways but always contains two essential comfort foods at its heart.

Makes 6 servings

Time: 45 minutes to 1 hour with precooked beans

5 tablespoons extra-virgin olive oil

1 large onion, chopped

2 teaspoons minced garlic

2 sprigs fresh rosemary or 1 teaspoon dried rosemary

3 cups drained cooked or canned kidney, cannellini, borlotti, or other beans or a mixture

2 cups cored, peeled, seeded, and diced tomatoes (canned are fine; include their juice)

6 to 8 cups Vegetable Stock (page 29), store-bought vegetable broth, or water

Salt and freshly ground black pepper to taste

1/2 pound tubettini or other small pasta (or larger pasta broken into bits)

1/2 cup minced fresh parsley leaves

1/2 cup freshly grated Parmesan cheese

1 Place 4 tablespoons of the olive oil in a large, deep saucepan or casserole and turn the heat to medium. A minute later, add the onion and half the garlic; cook until the onion softens, stirring occasionally, about 5 minutes.

2 Add the rosemary, beans, and tomatoes, and cook, stirring and mashing the tomatoes with your spoon, until the mixture is warm and the tomatoes begin to break down, about 10 minutes.

3 Add 6 cups of stock or water and a good amount of salt and pepper. Raise the heat to medium-high and bring to a boil. Turn the heat to medium-low and simmer for 10 minutes, stirring occasionally. (You may prepare the soup in advance up to this point. Cover, refrigerate for up to 2 days, and reheat before proceeding.)

4 Add the pasta, along with additional stock or water if necessary. Simmer until the pasta is nearly tender, 10 minutes or so. Add half the parsley and the remaining garlic and cook another 5 minutes, until the pasta is well done but not mushy.

5 Sprinkle with the remaining parsley and drizzle with the remaining olive oil. Serve, passing the Parmesan at the table.

Preparation Tip: A soup like this might traditionally be made with leftover bits of pasta—the ends of a number of boxes in the pantry. This is a good idea, just don't overdo it. Too much pasta will make the soup way too starchy—and if you're using long or big pasta, break it up before cooking.

Black Bean Soup

The best way to prepare this soup is to puree about half of it, then pour it back into the pot. But you can also mash the soup contents in the pot to get a similar smooth-chunky effect. For a vegan dish, omit the sour cream or yogurt.

Makes 4 to 6 servings

Time: 30 minutes with precooked beans

2 tablespoons canola or other neutral oil

2 medium onions, chopped

1 tablespoon minced garlic

1 tablespoon chili powder, or to taste

3 cups drained cooked black beans

4 cups Vegetable Stock (page 29), store-bought vegetable broth, or water, preferably warmed

Salt and freshly ground black pepper to taste

2 teaspoons freshly squeezed lime juice, or to taste

Sour cream or plain yogurt for garnish

Minced cilantro leaves for garnish

1 Place the oil in a large, deep saucepan or casserole and turn the heat to medium. A minute later, add the onions and cook, stirring, until softened, about 5 minutes. Stir in the garlic and chili powder and cook, stirring, another minute.

2 Add the beans and stock or water and season with salt and pepper. Turn the heat to medium-high and bring the soup just about to a boil. Turn the heat to medium-low, and cook, stirring occasionally, for about 10 minutes. Turn off the heat.

3 Force half the contents of the pot through a food mill or carefully puree it in a food processor or blender; or just mash the contents with a potato masher or large fork. (You may prepare the soup in advance up to this point. Cover, refrigerate for up to 2 days, and reheat before proceeding.)

4 Add the lime juice and stir; taste and adjust seasoning as necessary. Serve, garnished with sour cream or yogurt and minced cilantro.

3 Simple Vegetarian Additions to Bean Soups

1 Any spice you like, from jalapeños or other chiles to lots of black pepper to curry powder or other spice mixtures

2 Freshly chopped herbs or quick-cooking greens

3 Diced fresh tomatoes as a garnish

ⓥ Roasted Gazpacho

This is a complex, full-flavored gazpacho, a far cry from the pathetic blend often served in restaurants that more closely resembles tomato juice (or, at best, V-8). Practically a meal in itself, and especially good in August, when the vegetables are at their peak.

Makes 6 servings

Time: 45 minutes, plus time to chill

4 ripe tomatoes

2 small or 1 medium eggplant, peeled and cut into large chunks

4 small or 2 medium zucchini, cut into large chunks

2 medium onions, cut into large chunks

About 10 cloves garlic, peeled

½ cup extra-virgin olive oil

¼ cup sherry vinegar

Salt and freshly ground black pepper to taste

4 cups water

4 slices stale Italian or French bread, crusts removed and torn up

Baked Croutons (at right) for garnish (optional)

1 Preheat the oven to 400°F. Combine the tomatoes, eggplant, zucchini, onions, garlic, and olive oil in a large roasting pan; roast until the eggplant is tender, stirring occasionally, about 30 minutes.

2 Turn the mixture into a bowl and add the vinegar, salt, pepper, water, and bread. Refrigerate and let sit several hours or overnight.

3 In a food processor or blender, blend the mixture until smooth. Put it through a food mill or strainer to remove any remaining bits of skin, seeds, and other solids. Check the seasoning, garnish, and serve.

Baked Croutons

Makes about 2 cups cubes • Time: 20 to 40 minutes

If you like, rub the whole slices of bread with a cut clove of garlic before cooking. If you use a basic French baguette or other bread made only with flour, yeast, water, and salt, this is a vegan recipe. If you use sandwich bread or another bread made with butter, eggs, or other dairy, this won't be a vegan recipe.

4 to 6 slices any bread, preferably slightly stale

1 Preheat the oven to 300°F. Cut the bread into cubes of any size, or leave the slices whole. Place them on a baking sheet.

2 Bake, shaking the pan occasionally if you used cubes, or turning the slices every 10 minutes or so if you left the slices whole. The croutons are done when they are lightly browned and thoroughly dried. Store in a covered container at room temperature for up to a week.

4 Pasta

V Vegan

Linguine with Fresh Tomato Sauce and Parmesan

A seasonal dish, barely worth making unless the tomatoes are so good you'd eat them like apples. (The Parmesan must be high quality too.) This is my down-and-dirty version; it takes no time at all and is almost perfect, as long as you don't mind tomato skins. (If you do, follow the peeling directions in Steps 2 and 3 of the illustration at right.) The basil is optional; the sauce will be successful without it. But when you have fresh tomatoes, you can usually find fresh basil without trouble.

Makes about 4 servings

Time: 20 minutes

5 tablespoons butter

3 or 4 medium-to-large tomatoes, about 1 pound total, cored and roughly chopped

½ cup shredded fresh basil leaves

1 pound linguine

Salt and freshly ground black pepper to taste

Lots of freshly grated Parmesan cheese

1 Bring a large pot of water to a boil.

2 Melt 4 tablespoons of the butter in a medium-to-large skillet over medium heat. When the foam subsides, add the tomatoes.

3 Cook, stirring occasionally, until the tomatoes break up, about 10 minutes; fish the tomato skins from the sauce as they separate from the pulp (or leave them in if you're not after elegance). Add most of the basil, reserving some for garnish.

4 Meanwhile, salt the boiling water and cook the pasta until it is tender but firm. Season the sauce with salt and pepper; if it is thick—which it may be if you used meaty plum tomatoes or cooked out some of the liquid—thin it with some of the pasta cooking water. Drain the pasta and toss it with the sauce and remaining 1 tablespoon butter. Garnish with the reserved basil and serve with the Parmesan.

Garlicky Fresh Tomato Sauce In Step 2, cook 1 tablespoon or more minced garlic in the butter as it is heating over medium-low heat. When it just begins to color, raise the heat to medium and add the tomatoes. For even more garlic flavor, add another teaspoon of minced garlic no more than 1 or 2 minutes before the sauce is done.

Lower-Fat Fresh Tomato Sauce Replace the butter with just enough olive oil to film the bottom of the pan, 1 tablespoon or less. Use an extra tomato and finish with oil instead of butter.

Preparing Tomatoes

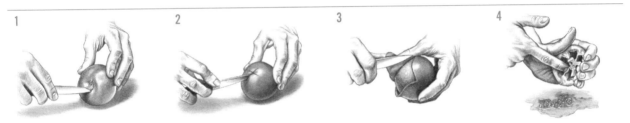

(Step 1) First, core the tomato. Cut a wedge right around the core and remove it. **(Step 2)** If desired, then peel the tomato. (If not, skip to Step 4.) Cut a small "x" in the flower (non-stem) end. Drop it into boiling water until the skin begins to loosen, usually less than thirty seconds. **(Step 3)** Remove the peels with a paring knife. **(Step 4)** Finish by seeding the tomato. The easiest way to remove seeds is to simply cut the tomato in half through its equator, then squeeze and shake out the seeds. Do this over a bowl if you wish to strain and reserve the juice.

Pasta with Basic Tomato Sauce

If you keep canned tomatoes on hand, you'll always be able to make fresh, delicious sauce in about the time it takes to bring water to a boil and cook the pasta. You can pass freshly grated cheese with this, but it is not essential.

Makes enough for at least 1 pound of pasta, about 4 servings

Time: 20 minutes

3 tablespoons olive oil

3 cloves garlic, lightly smashed,
or 1 small onion, minced

1 (28-ounce) can whole plum tomatoes

Salt and freshly ground black pepper
to taste

1 pound linguine or other long pasta

3 Vegetarian Ways to Vary Basic Tomato Sauce

1 Mozzarella Tomato Sauce: A kid-pleaser. Stir about 1 cup minced or grated mozzarella into the pasta with the sauce; this gives the pasta a pizza-like quality.

2 Puttanesca Sauce: Stir 2 tablespoons of capers (drained), some crushed red pepper flakes if you like, and/or ½ cup pitted black olives (the wrinkled, oil-cured type are best here) into the sauce after adding the tomatoes.

3 Mushroom Sauce: Add about 1 cup of reconstituted dried porcini, or 2 cups of fresh mushrooms, trimmed and chopped, or a combination to the oil, about 2 minutes after the garlic or onion. Cook for about 5 minutes, stirring, before adding the tomatoes.

1 Bring a large pot of water to a boil; salt it.

2 Warm 2 tablespoons of the oil with the garlic or onion in a medium skillet over medium-low heat. Cook, stirring occasionally, until the garlic is lightly golden or the onion is translucent.

3 Drain the tomatoes and remove their seeds if you choose to do so. Crush them with a fork or your hands and add them to the skillet, along with salt and pepper. Raise the heat to medium-high and cook, stirring occasionally, until the tomatoes break down and the mixture becomes "saucy," about 10 minutes. Remove the garlic if you like. Stir in the remaining tablespoon of oil, taste for salt, and add more if necessary. (This sauce may be covered and refrigerated for a day or two, or put in a closed container and frozen for several weeks.)

4 Meanwhile, cook the pasta until it is tender but firm. Ladle some of the cooking water into the sauce to thin it out a bit. Toss the pasta with the sauce and serve.

Penne Arrabbiata

This simple, "angry" pasta is a classic. But it is definitely a grown-up treat; it's too hot for most kids. Best served with grated Pecorino Romano cheese, which is stronger-tasting and saltier than Parmesan.

Makes about 4 servings

Time: 30 minutes

¼ cup olive oil

3 cloves garlic, cut into chunks or slices

3 or 4 small dried hot red chiles (or about 1 teaspoon crushed red pepper flakes)

1 (28-ounce) can whole plum tomatoes

Salt and freshly ground black pepper to taste

1 pound penne, ziti, or other cut pasta

¼ cup minced fresh parsley leaves

Grated Pecorino Romano (optional)

1 Bring a large pot of water to a boil.

2 Heat the olive oil, garlic, and chiles in a large skillet over medium-high heat. Cook, stirring occasionally, until the garlic becomes quite brown—but not black—7 or 8 minutes. Turn off the heat for 1 minute (this will reduce the spattering when you add the tomatoes).

3 Meanwhile, drain the tomatoes and remove their seeds if you choose to do so (page 41). Crush them with a fork or your hands and add them to the skillet, along with salt and pepper; turn the heat to medium. Cook, stirring occasionally, until the mixture becomes saucy, 10 to 15 minutes. Taste and adjust seasoning, if necessary. (This sauce may be covered and refrigerated for a day or 2, or put in a closed container and frozen for several weeks.)

4 Meanwhile, salt the boiling water and cook the pasta until it is tender but firm. When it is done, drain it and sauce it. Top with parsley and serve, with grated cheese if desired.

Pasta with Broccoli

You can take this preparation in a variety of directions (see the variation for one idea) but in any case it's a big, flavorful, filling dish which needs only bread to become a meal. Substitute cauliflower (or broccoflower) if you like, in either the main recipe or the variations.

Makes about 4 servings

Time: About 30 minutes

---

1 head broccoli, 1 pound or more
(see Tips on page 31)

¼ cup olive oil

1 tablespoon minced garlic

1 pound penne, ziti, or other cut pasta

Salt and freshly ground black pepper
to taste

Minced fresh parsley leaves for garnish

1 Bring a large pot of water to a boil; salt it.

2 Trim the broccoli and divide it into florets. Cook the broccoli in it until it is tender but not soft when pierced by a knife (the broccoli will cook further in the sauce, so be careful not to overcook it). Remove the broccoli and set it aside.

3 Meanwhile, cook the oil and garlic together in a large, deep skillet over medium-low heat, stirring occasionally. When the garlic is golden, turn off the heat if you're not ready to proceed.

4 Add the broccoli to the skillet and turn the heat to medium. Cook, stirring and mashing the broccoli, until it is hot and quite soft.

5 Meanwhile, cook the pasta. When the pasta is just about done, drain it, reserving about a cup of the cooking liquid. Add the pasta to the skillet with the broccoli and toss with a large spoon until well combined. Add salt and pepper, along with some of the pasta water to keep the mixture from drying out. Garnish and serve.

ⓥ Garlicky Pasta with Broccoli Raab

In Step 2, substitute for the broccoli 1 pound broccoli raab, roughly chopped into 1-inch pieces. Again, take care not to overcook it. Follow the master recipe. Mince an additional teaspoon or so of garlic and, in Step 5, add it to the broccoli along with the pasta. This is also good with a teaspoon or 2 of balsamic vinegar stirred into the mixture about a minute before serving.

Cooking Tips: There are times when the shape of pasta matters and times when it does not. Tiny morsels, for example, such as orzo, tubetti, and ditalini, are best in soups, because they fit on a spoon. Long pastas, like spaghetti and linguine, are best with sauces that don't have large chunks in them. Sauces with chunks should be served with bigger, tube-shaped pasta, such as penne, rigatoni, or ziti, or with shells and elbows.

That said, you shouldn't change the type of sauce you're making because you don't have the "correct" pasta shape. If you make spaghetti with a chunky sauce, some of the sauce will stay at the bottom of the bowl. This is less than ideal, of course, but you can eat that sauce with a spoon, or some bread.

Pasta with Saffron-Cauliflower Sauce

This is a Sicilian masterpiece, taught to me by my friend, chef Michael Lomonaco. Traditionally, the dish contains anchovies for flavor and richness, but I've left them out here to keep it vegetarian. The saffron, tomato, currants, and pine nuts combined provide great flavor. Lightly toast the pine nuts for added richness, if you like.

Makes about 4 servings

Time: About 40 minutes

1 head cauliflower, 1 pound or more

Several threads saffron

¼ cup olive oil

1 medium onion, finely chopped

1 tablespoon tomato paste

1 pound bucatini, perciatelli, or linguine

⅓ cup dried currants or raisins

¼ cup pine nuts

Salt and freshly ground black pepper to taste

1 Bring a large pot of water to a boil.

2 Trim the cauliflower and divide it into florets. Salt the water and cook the cauliflower in it until it is tender but not soft when pierced by a knife (the cauliflower will cook further in the sauce, so be careful not to overcook it). Remove the cauliflower and set it aside. Remove ¼ cup of the water and soak the saffron threads in it. Keep the water in the pot for the pasta and return to a boil.

3 Warm the olive oil for a minute in a large, deep skillet over medium heat. Add the onion and cook for 7 to 10 minutes, stirring, until translucent. Add the cauliflower florets, stir, and cook for 5 minutes. Add the saffron water, ½ cup of the cauliflower cooking water, and the tomato paste. Bring to a boil and reduce the heat to low.

4 Cook the pasta in the pot of boiling water. Add the currants and pine nuts to the sauce and season with salt and pepper.

5 When the pasta is done, drain and place in a large, warm serving bowl. Add half the cauliflower sauce and toss. Serve each portion with additional sauce on top.

Shopping Tip: There is real and fake saffron, the former from crocuses, the latter from marigolds. The difference is in cost and taste, and though real saffron is expensive, it's worth it. And, as it turns out, it isn't all that expensive per use. Buy an ounce from a reputable spice dealer for about $35 and if you use it wisely, it will last you 5 years.

Spaghetti with Eggplant

There are many ways to combine eggplant and pasta; my favorite begins with salting and sautéing, admittedly a chore. (The salting step can always be omitted, with a minor sacrifice in quality.) But well-sautéed eggplant is a creamy, savory treat, one that graces pasta beautifully. Still, there are less time-consuming alternatives; see the variations for a a couple.

Makes 4 servings

Time: 1½ hours, less if you choose not to salt the eggplant

---

2 small or 1 medium-to-large eggplant, about 1 pound total

Salt to taste

½ to ¾ cup olive oil

1 tablespoon minced garlic

½ teaspoon crushed red pepper flakes, or to taste

2 cups fresh or canned (drained) plum tomatoes, roughly chopped

1 pound spaghetti, linguine, or other long pasta

Minced fresh parsley leaves for garnish

1 Peel the eggplant if you like; cut it into ½-inch-thick or thinner slices, and salt and squeeze according to the directions on page 120.

2 Bring a large pot of water to a boil.

3 Place ¼ cup of oil in a large skillet and turn the heat to medium. When the oil shimmers, cook the eggplant slices in batches, without crowding, until nicely browned and tender, about 3 to 5 minutes per side. Regulate the heat so that the eggplant does not burn, and add additional oil as necessary. As the slices are cooked, set them on paper towels to remove excess oil.

4 When the eggplant is done, drain all but a film of oil from the skillet, and, with the heat still on medium, add the garlic and red pepper. Cook and stir for about 30 seconds, then add the tomatoes and salt. Cook, stirring occasionally, until the tomatoes break up and the mixture becomes saucy, 10 to 15 minutes. Meanwhile, salt the boiling water and cook the pasta. Cut the eggplant into strips.

5 When the sauce is done, taste it and adjust the seasoning, then stir half the eggplant into it. Drain the pasta when it is tender but firm and combine it with the sauce in a warm bowl. Top with the remaining eggplant, garnish, and serve.

Ⓥ Lower-Fat Pasta with Eggplant and Basil In Step 1, preheat the oven to 450°F. Cut the eggplant into small cubes or chunks ; salt and squeeze it if you have time. Toss it in a roasting pan or large ovenproof skillet with 1 tablespoon of oil, then roast it, shaking the pan occasionally, until tender, about 20 minutes. Meanwhile, heat 1 tablespoon of oil with 1 tablespoon of minced garlic in a large, deep skillet; add the tomatoes and cook as in Step 4, above. When the sauce is done, stir in the eggplant and ¼ cup shredded fresh basil leaves. Toss with the pasta and garnish with more basil.

Pasta Primavera

Primavera means "spring," but you can use a combination of vegetables from any season you like for this simple dish. Think of the ingredient list below as a "for instance."

Makes about 4 servings

Time: About 30 minutes

1½ cups **Vegetable Stock (page 29) or store-bought vegetable broth**

2 sprigs fresh thyme

Salt

½ cup peeled and diced carrot

1 cup asparagus tips, each about 1 inch long

½ cup diced zucchini or summer squash

½ cup shelled fresh or frozen peas, or snow peas

1 pound penne or other cut pasta

2 tablespoons extra-virgin olive oil or butter

Freshly ground black pepper to taste

1½ cups freshly grated Parmesan cheese

1 Bring a large pot of water to a boil.

2 Bring 1 cup of the stock to a boil in a medium skillet; add the thyme, and salt if necessary. Add the carrot and cook for 3 minutes. Add the asparagus tips and cook for 2 minutes. Add the zucchini and cook for 2 minutes. Add the peas and cook until all the vegetables are just tender, and the stock has just about evaporated. Turn off the heat.

3 Salt the boiling water and cook the pasta until it is tender but firm.

4 When the pasta is just about done, turn the heat under the vegetables to medium and stir in the olive oil or butter. Cook for about a minute, then add the remaining stock. Cook until the vegetables are very tender but not mushy.

5 Drain the pasta and toss it with the cooked vegetables and their broth; add salt and pepper to taste. Top with about a cup of Parmesan, or enough to thicken the sauce and serve, passing additional Parmesan at the table.

Spaghetti with Pesto

One of the fastest and easiest pasta sauces, assuming you have ready-made Pesto (see below) on hand.

Makes about 4 servings

Time: 20 minutes

1 pound spaghetti or other long pasta

2 tablespoons extra-virgin olive oil

1 cup Pesto (at right)

Freshly grated Parmesan cheese

1 Bring a large pot of water to a boil; salt it. Cook the pasta until it is tender but firm.

2 Meanwhile, stir the olive oil into the pesto to thin it a little. When the pasta is almost done, thin the pesto further with pasta cooking water, until it has the consistency of heavy cream.

3 Toss the pasta with the pesto, top with grated Parmesan, and serve, passing additional grated cheese at the table.

Shopping Tip: Olive oil is really the only all-purpose oil, and it's become increasingly easy to buy. The best is extra-virgin oil; technically it's defined by the amount of acid it contains, but you can think of it simply as the first, cold pressing of olives. There are no chemicals used in this process and the result, more often than not, is oil of distinctively fine character. It can be very expensive— $20 liter bottles are not uncommon—but it can also be reasonably priced at about $20 a gallon.

Pesto

Makes about 1 cup • Time: 5 minutes

You can make pesto thick or thin, according to your taste. Keep adding oil until you like the texture.

2 loosely packed cups fresh basil leaves, big stems discarded, rinsed, and dried

Salt to taste

1/2 to 2 cloves garlic, crushed

2 tablespoons pine nuts or walnuts, lightly toasted in a dry skillet

1/2 cup extra-virgin olive oil, or more

1/2 cup freshly grated Parmesan or other hard cheese (optional)

1 Combine the basil, salt, garlic, nuts, and about half the oil in a food processor or blender.

2 Process, stopping to scrape down the sides of the container occasionally, and adding the rest of the oil gradually. Add additional oil if you prefer a thinner mixture. Store in the refrigerator for a week or 2, or in the freezer for several months). Stir in the Parmesan by hand just before serving.

Pasta with Butter, Sage, and Parmesan

If you eliminate the sage, kids will love this dish. (There are homes in Italy where pasta with butter and Parmesan is the equivalent of pabulum.) But most grown-ups prefer the sharper edge that sage provides. Like many others, this sauce can be prepared in the time it takes water to boil.

Makes about 4 servings

Time: 30 minutes

6 tablespoons (¾ stick) butter

20 or 30 fresh sage leaves or about 1 tablespoon dried whole sage leaves

Salt and freshly ground black pepper to taste

1 pound cut pasta, such as ziti or penne, or long pasta, such as linguine or spaghetti

1 cup freshly grated Parmesan cheese

1 Bring a large pot of water to a boil.

2 Melt the butter in a small saucepan over low heat. Add the sage, salt, and pepper. Cook until the butter turns light brown, about 10 minutes.

3 Salt the boiling water and cook the pasta until it is tender but firm. Spoon 2 or 3 tablespoons of the pasta cooking water into a warm serving bowl. Drain the pasta and toss in the serving bowl with the butter, more pepper, and half the Parmesan. Pass the remaining Parmesan at the table.

Eggplant Lasagne

Vegetarian lasagne can be made quite simply, with nothing more than a layer of noodles, some cheese, and a sauce. But because most people think of it as a hearty, special occasion dish, I like to combine two sauces—béchamel and tomato—and a layer of crisp-cooked eggplant. The results are nothing short of spectacular.

Makes about 6 servings

Time: 45 minutes (with premade sauce)

2 medium-to-large eggplant, about 2 pounds

Salt

At least 5 quarts water

1/2 cup extra-virgin olive oil, more or less

12 fresh or dried lasagne noodles

1 recipe Béchamel Sauce (at right), about 1 1/2 cups

2 tablespoons softened butter (preferred) or extra-virgin olive oil

3 cups, more or less, Basic Tomato Sauce or Mushroom Sauce (#3 from list of variations, page 42)

1 1/2 cups freshly grated Parmesan cheese

Freshly ground black pepper to taste

1 Peel the eggplant if you like; cut it the long way into 1/4-inch-thick slices, and salt and squeeze according to the directions on page 120. Set at least 5 quarts of water in a large pot over high heat. When it comes to a boil, salt it.

2 Put 1/4 cup of oil in a large skillet and turn the heat to medium. When the oil shimmers, cook the eggplant slices in batches, without crowding, until nicely browned and tender, about 3 to 5 minutes per side. Regulate the heat so that the eggplant does not burn, and add additional oil as necessary. As the slices are cooked, set them on paper towels to remove excess oil.

3 If you are using fresh pasta, roll it out. Assuming your baking pan is 9 inches across and 13 inches long, make your pasta ribbons 26 inches long, then cut them in half. You will still need to cut the noodles so that they fit reasonably snugly into your pan.

4 Cook the noodles a few at a time; keep them underdone (if they are fresh, this means little more than a minute of cooking time). Drain carefully in a colander, then allow to rest on towels while you prepare the Béchamel Sauce. Preheat the oven to 400°F.

5 Smear the bottom of your baking pan with the butter or oil, then place a layer of noodles, touching but not overlapping. Trim any overhanging edges. Cover the noodles with about 1/4 each of the béchamel, tomato sauce, some eggplant, and Parmesan, then with a light sprinkling of black pepper (between the tomato sauce and the Parmesan, there should be enough salt, but if you feel it is underseasoned, add a little salt to each

layer also). Make 3 or 4 layers, ending with a sprinkling of Parmesan. (The dish can be prepared in advance up to this point, then well-wrapped and refrigerated for a day or frozen for a month; defrost in the refrigerator for a day before cooking, if possible.)

6 Bake for about 20 to 30 minutes, until the lasagne is bubbly. Remove from the oven and let rest for 5 minutes before cutting and serving. Or let cool completely, cover well, and refrigerate for up to 2 days, or freeze for up to a month.

Béchamel (Milk) Sauce
Makes about 1½ cups • Time: 10 to 20 minutes

Béchamel sauce is a basic French white sauce made with milk, butter, and flour. It can be served over simply cooked vegetables, and it is also used for classic lasagne by cooks in Bologna, where it is called *besciamella*.

1½ tablespoons butter	1½ cups milk, warmed
1½ tablespoons flour	Salt and freshly ground black pepper to taste

1 In a small saucepan, heat the butter over medium-low heat. When the foam begins to subside, stir in the flour. Turn the heat to low and cook, stirring with a wire whisk almost constantly, until the flour-butter mixture darkens, at least 3 minutes.

2 Stir in the milk, a little bit at a time, still using the whisk. When about a cup of the milk has been stirred in, the mixture will be fairly thick. Add more milk, a little at a time, until the consistency is just a little thinner than you like, then cook, still over low heat, until the mixture is the thickness you want.

3 Season to taste and serve immediately or keep warm over gently simmering water for up to an hour, stirring occasionally.

3 Ideas for Vegetarian Lasagne

You can employ these ideas singly or in combination.

1 Add a layer or two of sliced, sautéed vegetables such as mushrooms, zucchini, or cauliflower.

2 Add a layer of strong cheese, such as Gorgonzola.

3 Add fresh herbs, especially basil (whole leaves are nice) or chopped parsley.

Stir-Fried Chinese Noodles with Vegetables

You can make Chinese-style stir-fried noodles with dried wheat or rice noodles, or with fresh egg noodles. And this recipe can be made with virtually any green vegetable. For example, I've used asparagus; substitute at will, making sure the vegetable is cut into bite-sized pieces and cooked until tender before proceeding. If you'd like to use sautéed rather than parboiled vegetables, see the variation on page 53. You can also combine these noodles with almost any stir-fried dish.

Makes about 4 servings

Time: 20 to 30 minutes

1 pound asparagus, more or less, no thicker than a pencil

1 pound Chinese wheat noodles, of spaghetti-like thickness

3 tablespoons peanut (preferred) or other oil

1 tablespoon minced garlic

1 tablespoon peeled and minced fresh ginger

1/2 cup Vegetable Stock (page 29), store-bought vegetable broth, or reserved cooking water

1 tablespoon soy sauce

1/4 cup minced scallion or chives

1 tablespoon dark sesame oil (optional)

1 Bring a large pot of water to a boil; salt it. Meanwhile, break the bottoms of the asparagus (they usually snap right at the point where the stalk is tender enough to eat); cut them into 1- to 2-inch lengths. When the pot of water is boiling, blanch the asparagus just until they begin to become tender, 1 to 3 minutes depending on their thickness. Remove them from the water with a slotted spoon and quickly plunge into ice water to stop the cooking.

2 Using the same water, cook the noodles, stirring occasionally and beginning to taste after 4 or 5 minutes (less time if you're using fresh noodles). When they are just tender, drain thoroughly, reserving 1/2 cup cooking liquid if you do not have any stock. Toss with a tablespoon of the oil (a little more if you are not proceeding with the recipe right away), and set aside.

3 Just before you are ready to eat, heat a large skillet or wok (preferably non-stick) over medium-high heat for 3 or 4 minutes. Add the remaining oil, then the garlic and ginger; let sizzle for about 15 seconds, then toss in the noodles. Raise the heat to high and let the noodles sit for about a minute, until they begin to brown on the bottom. Toss once or twice and allow to sit again. Add the stock or cooking water and stir, scraping to loosen any bits that may have stuck to the bottom. Add the (drained) asparagus and stir a few times; add the soy sauce and scallion or chives and the sesame oil if you are using it. Stir and serve.

Ⓥ Stir-Fried Noodles with Stir-Fried Vegetables Omit asparagus. Use about 1 pound of tender vegetables, such as spring onions, leeks, broccoli raab, celery, bean sprouts, napa cabbage, bok choy, snow peas, or a combination. Trim and chop into small pieces if necessary; cook them in a large non-stick skillet or wok over high heat with 2 or 3 tablespoons of peanut oil. Stir every 10 seconds or so until vegetables are brown and tender. Cook the noodles as in Step 2, then substitute this mixture for the asparagus in Step 3.

3 Vegetarian Additions to Stir-Fried Noodles

Chinese noodles, like Italian pasta, are a catch-all for anything that seems appropriate. Here are some ideas:

1 Any leftover cooked vegetable, rinsed of seasonings with boiling water if necessary, cut into bite-sized pieces

2 Any raw vegetable, cut into small pieces and parboiled or briefly stir-fried

3 Almost any spice: toasted, ground Szechwan peppercorns; a table-spoon or two of hoisin, oyster, plum, or ground bean sauce; curry or five-spice powder to taste

Japanese udon noodles have a slightly different texture than the wheat noodles of other countries, but you can substitute Chinese wheat noodles or Italian pasta—spaghetti, capellini, linguine, or fettuccine are the best shapes. Somen noodles are also good in this stock, but be especially careful not to overcook them. The stock in this dish is traditionally dashi—a stock made with a fish base—but you'll get nice flavor with vegetable stock, too.

This is a dish that can take many, many different directions. The variation is just one possibility.

Makes about 4 servings

Time: 20 minutes

1 pound udon (Japanese wheat) or soba (buckwheat) noodles

4 cups Vegetable Stock (page 29) or store-bought broth

⅓ cup mild soy sauce

⅓ cup mirin (Japanese sweet rice wine)

1 tablespoon sugar

Salt, if needed

½ cup finely minced scallions

1 tablespoon peeled and grated fresh ginger (optional)

1　Bring a large pot of water to a boil. Salt the water and cook the noodles until they are just tender—a little bit underdone. Drain and rinse them with cold water.

2　While the noodles are cooking, heat the stock and add to it the soy sauce, mirin, and sugar; stir to combine. Taste and add salt if necessary. Keep the stock hot but do not let it boil. When the noodles are done, reheat them gently in the stock, then ladle portions of noodles and soup into individual bowls. Garnish with the scallions and ginger if you like, and serve immediately.

Ⓥ Japanese Noodles with Shiitakes and Sesame Step 1 remains the same. Soak 2 or 3 dried shiitake (also called black) mushrooms in hot water for 10 minutes. Add the soaking liquid to the stock in Step 2, trim the mushrooms of any hard spots, then cut them into thin slices. Add them to the stock and proceed as above. When the noodles and stock are combined, drizzle with 1 tablespoon dark sesame oil. For the scallions, substitute ⅓ cup lightly toasted sesame seeds; the ginger remains optional.

Pad Thai

This Pad Thai is a vegetarian version of the classic Thai fried noodle dish, which normally includes shrimp and Asian fish sauce. It is packed with strong flavors: It's sweet, sour, spicy, even a little hot. Once you've soaked the rice noodles and assembled the ingredients, this will take you less than 10 minutes to cook.

Makes 4 servings

Time: About 45 minutes, including time to soak the noodles

12 ounces rice noodles, preferably vermicelli

3 tablespoons peanut (preferred) or other oil

3 or 4 dried shiitake ("black") mushrooms

2 tablespoons minced garlic

1/2 cup scallions, trimmed and cut into 1-inch sections

1/4 cup roasted salted peanuts (unchopped)

2 eggs, lightly beaten

2 tablespoons soy sauce

1 tablespoon sugar

Salt, if needed

1 1/2 cups mung bean sprouts

1/4 cup roasted salted peanuts, chopped

1/2 teaspoon crushed red pepper flakes, or to taste

Minced cilantro leaves

2 limes or lemons, quartered

1 Soak the noodles in warm water to cover until soft; this will take from 15 to 30 minutes. You can change the water once or twice to hasten the process slightly. Drain thoroughly, then toss with half the oil. Meanwhile, soak the mushrooms in hot water for about 10 minutes; trim off any hard spots and chop.

2 Heat the remaining oil over medium-high heat in a wok or large, deep non-stick skillet, for a minute or so, until the first wisp of smoke appears. Add the garlic and cook, stirring, for 30 seconds. Add the mushrooms, scallions, and unchopped peanuts. Cook for about 2 minutes.

3 Add the eggs and let sit for 15 seconds or so, until they begin to set. Then scramble with the mushrooms and garlic, breaking up any large clumps. Add the soy sauce and sugar and cook, stirring, for 15 seconds. Add the noodles and toss and cook until heated through. Taste and add salt as needed. Add 1 cup of bean sprouts and toss to distribute through the noodles.

4 Turn the noodles out onto a platter and garnish with the remaining bean sprouts, the chopped peanuts, a sprinkling of crushed red pepper flakes, and some cilantro. Squeeze some lemon or lime juice over all and serve, passing more lemon or lime separately.

Preparation Tip: If you have a few days, you can make your own bean sprouts: Rinse 1/2 cup whole mung beans with water, then soak for 6 to 12 hours. Put in a jar or bowl that you can cover with a piece of cheesecloth or a very coarse napkin. Drain, rinse, and drain them again. Prop the jar up so that it is on its side with the mouth tilted down. Shield from the light with the cheesecloth. Rinse and drain at least twice a day. After a couple of days, the seeds will have sprouted. When the sprouts are the length you want them, rinse one more time and expose to the light for a few hours; this will turn the sprouts green.

5 | Grains

Ⓥ Vegan

Precooked Rice or Other Grains with Garlic or Onions

You can change the flavor of this dish by substituting minced shallots (about ¼ cup) or chopped leeks (about ½ cup) for the garlic or onion. (Leave out the butter for a vegan dish.)

Makes 4 servings

Time: 15 to 20 minutes

3 tablespoons olive oil, butter, or a combination

1 tablespoon minced garlic, or to taste, or ½ cup chopped onion

3 to 4 cups precooked grains (at right), such as rice or barley

Salt and freshly ground black pepper to taste

Minced fresh parsley leaves for garnish

1　Combine the oil and/or butter and the garlic or onion in a large skillet, preferably non-stick, and turn the heat to medium-low. Cook, stirring occasionally, just until the garlic or onion softens and begins to brown, 5 to 10 minutes.

2　Add the grains and cook, stirring occasionally, until heated through, about 10 minutes.

3　Season with salt and pepper, garnish, and serve.

Shopping Tip: Most grains, even when processed to remove their hulls, or lightly precooked in the traditional style (as are bulgur and kasha), retain most of their natural oils, so buying them as fresh as possible is key to avoiding rancidity. Buy them in bulk, from a place with fast turnover. That may mean a specialty store (for instance, you can get great bulgur in a Middle Eastern store) or a natural foods store.

Preparation Tips: Once grains are in your home, you can store them in the refrigerator, but if there is room in the freezer, that's even better; there's no need to defrost before cooking.

Most grains (bulgur and kasha are the exceptions) should be rinsed before cooking.

Ⓥ Precooked Rice or Other Grains with Mushrooms In Step 1, add 1 cup trimmed and chopped mushrooms, along with the garlic or onion. Cook, stirring occasionally, until the mushrooms are softened and begin to brown, 5 to 10 minutes. Add the grains and finish as above.

Ⓥ Precooked Rice or Other Grains with Toasted Nuts or Seeds In Step 1, add 1/2 cup roughly chopped (but not minced) cashews, walnuts, unsalted (preferably raw) peanuts, blanched almonds, sunflower seeds, or toasted, shelled pumpkin seeds (pepitas) after the garlic or onions soften. Cook, stirring frequently, until they begin to brown, about 3 minutes. Add the grains and finish as above.

Ⓥ Precooked Rice or Other Grains with Pesto Follow the original recipe to the end, then stir 1/2 cup basic Pesto (page 48), or to taste, into the grains. Garnish, if possible, with chopped fresh basil.

Ⓥ Simple Precooked Rice or Other Grains

Makes 4 servings • Time: 10 minutes to more than 1 hour, depending on the grain

Many grains can be prepared with this technique, an easy way to get the flavor, satisfying substance, and nutrients they provide. Try it with long-grain white rice; brown rice; pearled barley; whole wheat (wheat berries) and whole rye (rye berries), preferably after dry-toasting in a skillet, followed by an overnight soaking in water to cover; hominy (*pozole*); and wild rice. The grains can be served as is with beans, vegetables, or other flavorful dishes, or enhanced as in the previous recipe.

At least 6 cups water	**1 1/2 cups any grain listed above,**
Salt	**rinsed**

1 Bring at least 6 cups water to a boil in a medium-to-large pot; salt it. Stir in the grain and adjust the heat so that the water boils, but not furiously.

2 Cook, stirring occasionally, until the grain is tender. This will take about 7 or 8 minutes with some white rice, and as long as 1 hour or more for some brown rice, unpearled barley, wheat berries, and other unhulled grains. Add additional boiling water if necessary to keep grains covered.

3 Pour the grain into a strainer; plunge the strainer into ice-cold water to stop the cooking. Drain again, or refrigerate for later use.

Basic Long-Grain Rice

Cooking rice is easy. Just be sure to use gentle heat once the water comes to a boil. If the pot dries out before the rice is tender, add a couple of tablespoons of hot or boiling water and re-cover.

Makes 4 servings

Time: About 20 minutes

1½ cups long-grain rice

2¼ cups Vegetable Stock (page 29), store-bought vegetable broth, or water

1 teaspoon salt, or to taste

1 Combine the rice, liquid, and salt in a medium saucepan and turn the heat to medium-high. Bring to a boil.

2 Turn the heat to medium-low and cover. Cook for 15 minutes, or until the water is absorbed and the rice is tender. At this point:

- If the water is not absorbed but the rice is tender, uncover and raise the heat a bit. Cook, stirring (you can add a little butter or oil if you like to prevent sticking), until the liquid evaporates.

- If the water is not absorbed and the rice is not yet tender, re-cover and check in 3 minutes.

- If the water is absorbed and the rice is not yet tender, add a few tablespoons of hot or boiling liquid, re-cover, and check in 3 minutes.

Shopping Tip: There are essentially two kinds of rice: long and short grain. Long-grain rice cooks in separate, firm, dry kernels; short-grain (and so-called medium-grain) rice cooks up soft, moist, and a little sticky. Basmati is the best tasting long-grain specialty rice. Jasmine rice is also long grain, and also aromatic. But it cooks as if it were short grain; that is, moist and somewhat sticky. It has a wonderful aroma and flavor, and is associated with Thai food.

Ⓥ Basic Brown Rice

Makes 4 servings • Time: About 45 minutes

Long-grain brown rice is easier to cook by the method on page 59 (Simple Precooked Grains), although this technique works fine. I do prefer this method for short- or medium-grain brown rice, which you want a little on the sticky side.

1 cup any brown rice, rinsed	Salt and freshly ground black pepper to taste
2½ cups Vegetable Stock (page 29), store-bought vegetable broth, or water, plus more if needed	1 tablespoon butter, or more to taste (optional)

1 Combine the first three ingredients in a medium saucepan and bring to a boil over medium-high heat.

2 Cover, turn the heat to low, and cook, undisturbed, for 40 minutes. Check the rice: It is done when it is quite tender and all the liquid has been absorbed. If the rice is not quite done, continue to cook, adding a tablespoon or 2 more liquid if all the liquid has been absorbed. Or, if the rice is tender but a little liquid remains, simply cover and turn off the heat; the rice will absorb the liquid within 10 minutes. If ¼ cup or more of water remains (unlikely), uncover and raise the heat a bit; cook, stirring, until the rice is fluffy and the liquid has evaporated.

3 Serve, with butter if you like.

Ⓥ Rice Pilaf

There are many definitions of pilaf, but two are common to all: The rice must be briefly cooked in oil or butter before adding liquid, and the liquid must be flavorful. The oil or butter may be flavored with vegetables, herbs, or spices; the liquid may be anything from lobster stock to yogurt; and other foods may be added to the pot.

Makes 4 servings

Time: About 30 minutes

2 tablespoons oil or butter

1 cup chopped onion

1½ cups long-grain rice

Salt and freshly ground black pepper

2½ cups Vegetable Stock (page 29), store-bought vegetable broth, or water, heated to the boiling point

Minced fresh parsley leaves for garnish

1 Place the oil or butter in a large, deep skillet which can later be covered and turn the heat to medium-high. When the oil is hot or the butter melts, add the onion. Cook, stirring, until the onion softens but does not begin to brown, 5 to 8 minutes.

2 Add the rice all at once, turn the heat to medium, and stir until the rice is glossy and completely coated with oil or butter, 2 or 3 minutes. Season well, then turn the heat down to low and add the liquid, all at once. Cover the pan.

3 Cook for 15 minutes, then check the rice. When the rice is tender and the liquid is absorbed, it's done. If not, cook for 2 or 3 minutes and check again. Check the seasoning, garnish, and serve immediately.

Ⓥ **Pilaf with Currants and Pine Nuts** Along with the rice, add ¼ cup currants (or raisins), 2 tablespoons pine nuts, and ½ teaspoon cinnamon. Proceed as above.

Ⓥ **Pilaf with Chickpeas or Peas** Just before adding the stock or water, stir in 1 cup cooked chickpeas or raw green peas (frozen are okay, and you need not defrost first). Proceed as above.

Ⓥ **Golden Pilaf** Before adding the stock, warm it with a large pinch (¼ to ½ teaspoon) saffron threads.

Ⓥ Coconut Rice

A simple and wonderful side dish, essential in the cuisines of the Caribbean. It's so much more delicious than plain rice—and not much more difficult to make—that you may make it your basic rice dish.

Makes 3 to 4 servings

Time: 20 minutes

1 tablespoon peanut (preferred)
or vegetable oil

1 cup long-grain white rice

Salt and freshly ground black pepper
to taste

2 cups canned or Fresh Coconut Milk
(page 79), warmed

1 Place the oil in a medium saucepan over medium heat. Stir in the rice and cook, stirring, until it becomes translucent, about 2 minutes. Season with salt and pepper and stir in the coconut milk.

2 Bring to a boil, turn the heat to low, cover, and cook for about 15 minutes, or until all the liquid is absorbed. The rice can rest, covered, for 10 to 15 minutes before serving.

Ⓥ **Coconut Rice with Beans** Stir in 1/2 to 1 cup cooked pinto, kidney, or other red beans along with the coconut milk. Add a pinch of allspice, 1/2 teaspoon ground cinnamon, or 1 teaspoon minced fresh oregano or marjoram or 1/2 teaspoon dried.

Ⓥ **Coconut Rice with Chipotles** Soak 2 dried chipotle chiles (or to taste) in 1 cup very hot water. Stem, seed, and mince them when they are softened. Add them to the pot along with the rice in Step 1. Proceed as above.

Fried Rice with Egg

Leftover rice is ideal for fried rice, and this simple, basic version is one you can build on. Add any other minced cooked vegetables you like.

Makes 4 servings

Time: 20 minutes or less with precooked rice

3 tablespoons peanut (preferred) or canola or other oil

1 teaspoon minced garlic

1 teaspoon peeled and minced fresh ginger

2 tablespoons chopped scallion, plus minced scallion for garnish

3 to 4 cups leftover or cooked rice (any method is fine), cooled

2 eggs, lightly beaten

2 tablespoons soy sauce

Salt and freshly ground black pepper to taste

1 Place the oil in a wok or large skillet, preferably non-stick, and turn the heat to high. A minute later, add the garlic, ginger, and chopped scallion and cook, stirring almost constantly, for 1 minute.

2 Turn the heat down a little bit and add the rice, a little bit at a time, crumbling it with your fingers to eliminate lumps if necessary. Stir frequently for about 3 minutes.

3 Make a little hole in the center of the rice and pour in the eggs. Scramble, incorporating them gradually with the rice as you bring bits of the rice back to the center.

4 Add the soy sauce and stir. Add salt and pepper if necessary. Garnish and serve.

Tofu Fried Rice with Peas In Step 2, after adding the rice, stir in about 1 cup chopped firm tofu and 1/2 cup briefly cooked peas (fresh or frozen). Proceed as above; the eggs are optional.

Brown Rice with Cashews and Herbs

A wonderfully chewy side dish; substitute other nuts for the cashews if you like.

Makes 4 servings

Time: About 45 minutes

2 tablespoons olive or other oil or butter

1 medium onion, chopped

1 teaspoon minced garlic

1 cup any brown rice, rinsed

1/2 cup cashew pieces

1 bay leaf

1/2 teaspoon fresh thyme leaves
or 1/4 teaspoon dried thyme

Salt and freshly ground black pepper

2 cups Vegetable Stock (page 29),
store-bought broth, or water

Minced fresh parsley leaves for garnish

1 Place the oil or butter in a medium-to-large skillet over medium heat; when the oil is hot or the butter melts, add the onion and garlic and cook, stirring, until softened, about 5 minutes.

2 Add the brown rice and nuts and cook, stirring, for 1 minute; add the herbs, salt, pepper, and liquid. Bring to a boil.

3 Turn the heat to low, cover, and cook for 30 minutes. Check the rice's progress: It is done when tender but still a little chewy. Continue to cook if necessary, adding a tablespoon or two more liquid if all the liquid has been absorbed and the rice is not quite done. Or, if the rice is tender but a little liquid remains, simply cover and turn off the heat; the rice will absorb the liquid within 10 minutes. If 1/4 cup or more of water remains (unlikely), uncover and raise the heat a bit; cook, stirring, until the rice is tender and the liquid is evaporated. Remove the bay leaf. Garnish and serve.

Bulgur Pilaf with Vermicelli

Heavenly with butter, wonderful with oil, this is among the best side dishes there is, and a good way to use up odd bits of noodles. If you don't have vermicelli, use any long pasta. If you only have cut pasta, such as ziti or shells, put it in a plastic bag and smack it a few times with a rolling pin or skillet to break it into smaller pieces. (See page 23, Tabbouleh, for more info about bulgur.)

Makes 4 servings

Time: 30 minutes

4 tablespoons (½ stick) butter
or extra-virgin olive oil

2 medium onions or 1 large onion,
chopped

½ cup vermicelli, broken into
2-inch-long or shorter lengths,
or other pasta

1 cup medium-grind (Number 2)
or coarse-grind (Number 3) bulgur

Salt and freshly ground black pepper
to taste

1 tablespoon tomato paste (optional)

2¼ cups Vegetable Stock (page 29),
store-bought vegetable broth, or water,
preferably warmed

1 Place the butter or oil in a medium skillet or saucepan that can later be covered and turn the heat to medium. Add the onion and cook, stirring, until it is soft, about 5 minutes.

2 Add the vermicelli and the bulgur and cook, stirring, until coated with butter or oil. Add all the remaining ingredients, turn the heat to low, and cover. Cook for 10 minutes, then turn off the heat and let sit for 15 minutes more. Adjust the seasoning and serve.

Polenta

You can spend more time making polenta if you like. But as long as you use enough water, 15 minutes of stirring is usually sufficient, although cooking time is to some extent dependent on the consistency you are trying to achieve, which in turn determines the amount of water you use (see the recipe). Of course, adding plenty of butter and cheese at the end of cooking helps matters along.

Makes 4 servings

Time: About 30 minutes

4 cups water (5 if you would like very soft polenta; 3½ if you plan to spread and cut the polenta)

1 teaspoon salt, plus more if necessary

1 cup medium-grind cornmeal (see Tip)

Freshly ground black pepper to taste

2 tablespoons butter (optional)

¼ cup or more freshly grated Parmesan or crumbled Gorgonzola cheese (optional)

Snipped fresh chives or dill or minced fresh parsley leaves for garnish

1 Bring the water to a boil in a heavy medium pot, preferably non-stick; salt it and turn the heat to medium. Add the cornmeal a little bit at a time, whisking constantly with a wire whisk. Once you've whisked in all the cornmeal, turn the heat to low.

2 Cook, whisking every minute for the first 5 minutes, then switching to a flat-bottomed wooden spoon. Stir frequently, almost constantly, until all the water is absorbed. Soft polenta should be creamy; firmer polenta, such as that needed for slicing and grilling, should begin to pull away from the sides of the pot. This will take about 15 minutes with the minimum amount of water and 30 to 40 with the maximum. Turn off the heat; taste and add more salt if necessary, along with some pepper.

3 Stir in the optional butter and cheese and stir until they dissolve. Garnish and serve immediately, passing more cheese at the table, if you like.

Shopping Tip: Many Italian stores and supermarkets sell instant polenta, which is easy to make—and not bad, but not great. Short on taste, too, are the mass-produced commercial cornmeals sold in supermarkets, although "stone-ground" cornmeal sold in the baking aisles can be good. I recommend fresh stone-ground cornmeal from a natural foods store; store it in the freezer. Medium-grind cornmeal is best for both flavor and texture; although it takes a little longer to cook, it's worth the time.

Couscous with Raisins and Pine Nuts

There's a traditional method of preparing couscous, which involves moistening the couscous, then resting it, steaming it, moistening it again, salting it, cooling it, steaming it once more, then finally serving it with a stew. Most highly dedicated cooks try that method at least once, but it is a big production. This is a basic couscous recipe, using precooked or instant couscous, in which you can feel free to vary seasonings to your taste. Serve couscous with any moist stew or other dish with plenty of gravy; as a form of pasta—it isn't really a grain at all—it does not have a lot of flavor of its own.

Makes 4 servings

Time: About 15 minutes

2¼ cups Vegetable Stock (page 29), store-bought vegetable broth, or water

1 cinnamon stick

5 cardamom pods

Salt and freshly ground black pepper to taste

⅓ cup raisins or minced dried fruit such as apricots or figs, or a combination

⅓ cup hot water or stock

4 tablespoons (½ stick) butter

½ cup pine nuts

1½ cups couscous

Minced fresh parsley or cilantro leaves for garnish

1   In a small saucepan, warm the 2¼ cups stock with the cinnamon, cardamom, salt, and pepper while you prepare the other ingredients. Soak the raisins in the ⅓ cup hot water or stock.

2   Place 1 tablespoon butter in a small skillet and turn the heat to medium. When it melts, add the pine nuts and cook, stirring occasionally, until they brown lightly, about 5 minutes. Set aside.

3   Place 2 tablespoons butter in a medium saucepan and turn the heat to medium-low. When it melts, add the couscous and cook, stirring, until it is coated with butter, about 1 minute. Strain the stock or water and add it all at once. Bring to a boil, then turn the heat down to its minimum. Cover and cook until all the liquid is absorbed, 5 to 8 minutes. Drain the raisins and gently stir them in, along with the pine nuts and remaining butter. Fluff with a fork to break up any lumps. Garnish and serve.

Shopping Tip: Whole spices keep longer and, once ground, have more intense flavor than pre-ground spices. Generally speaking, it's best to toast them before grinding—just cook them in a dry skillet until they become fragrant, a couple of minutes—then grind in a spice or coffee grinder.

16 Grain, Bean, or Vegetable Dishes That Can Be Served as a Main Course

With a side dish, salad, or bread, all of these make not only adequate but wonderful center-of-the-table presentations.

6 | Beans

Ⓥ Vegan

Ⓥ Basic Beans

It's best to precook beans whenever you can because, unfortunately, precise timing is nearly impossible. A small white bean from a recent harvest may cook twice as fast—may be done in 30 minutes, in fact—as one that's been sitting on your shelf for more than a year and may in fact be two years old. So allow enough time unless you've cooked beans from the same batch before and can predict cooking time. Cooked beans store well, in their own liquid, in the refrigerator or freezer, and reheat perfectly on the stove top, in the oven, or in a microwave.

Time: 30 minutes to 2 hours,
largely unattended

Any quantity dried beans, washed and picked over (see Tips, at right)

Salt to taste

1   Place the beans in a large pot with water to cover. Turn the heat to high and bring to a boil; skim the foam if necessary. Turn the heat down so the beans simmer. Cover loosely.

2   Cook, stirring occasionally, until the beans begin to become tender; add about 1 teaspoon salt per ½ pound of beans, or to taste.

3   Continue to cook, stirring gently, until the beans are as tender as you like; add additional water if necessary. Drain and serve, or use in other recipes, or store covered, in their cooking liquid, in the refrigerator (3 days) or freezer (3 months).

Ⓥ **Slightly Faster Beans** You can speed the cooking process a little bit by thinking ahead. Soak the beans for at least 6 hours in water to cover, drain, then cook in fresh water. Or boil the beans for 2 minutes in water to cover, then soak them for 2 hours in that water, drain, then cook in fresh water. Either of these techniques usually reduces cooking time by 25 to 50 percent, or 15 to 30 minutes.

Shopping Tips: There is a difference between fresh and stale beans: newer beans taste better, cook faster, and contain more nutrients. Go to a place where there is a fair amount of turnover—a natural foods store, for example, or a Latino market. Your supermarket may sell a lot of beans these days, so you might start there, but if it seems that the beans you buy take longer to cook than you might expect given my guidelines, try buying them elsewhere.

Generally, beans should look consistent, and have deep, somewhat glossy color; faded, dry-looking beans are likely to be older, and those that are starting to wrinkle are not worth buying.

Preparation Tips: Store beans in covered containers or thick plastic bags in a dry place. I finish all the beans I've accumulated during the course of the year each summer, so that I know that I don't keep any longer than a year.

Sort through beans just before soaking or cooking: Put the beans in a pot and fill it with water, then swish the whole thing around while looking into the pot. Remove any beans that are discolored, shriveled, or broken and remove any pebbles or other stray matter. Then dump the beans into a colander and rinse for a minute or so.

Cooking Tip: Salt beans halfway through cooking, after they have begun to tenderize. Don't wait until they are done to add salt or they will be bland.

Ⓥ White Beans, Tuscan Style

The classic, simple, and always delicious beans of Tuscany. Great olive oil makes a big difference here. Add some cooked sausage and sautéed red bell peppers to make this into a simple main course.

Makes 4 servings

Time: 1 to 2 hours, largely unattended

About ½ pound dried white beans: cannellini, navy, great Northern, etc., washed and picked over (see Tips, page 73)

20 fresh sage leaves or 1 tablespoon dried sage

Salt and freshly ground black pepper to taste

2 teaspoons minced garlic

2 tablespoons extra-virgin olive oil

1 Place the beans in a pot with water to cover. Turn the heat to high and bring to a boil. Add the sage; adjust the heat so the beans simmer. Cover loosely.

2 Cook, stirring occasionally, until the beans begin to soften; add about ½ teaspoon salt and some pepper. Continue to cook until the beans are very tender; add additional water if the beans dry out.

3 Drain the cooking liquid if necessary, then add the garlic, along with some more salt and pepper if necessary. Stir in the olive oil and serve.

Beans and Greens

Best with white beans, whether small or large. Cook them until they are just about falling apart; these should be very creamy.

Makes 4 servings

Time: 1 to 2 hours, largely unattended

½ pound dried white beans, washed and picked over (see Tips, page 73)

1 medium onion, unpeeled

1 bay leaf

1 clove

Salt and freshly ground black pepper to taste

1½ pounds dark greens, such as kale, collards, mustard, or broccoli raab, well washed and roughly chopped

1 tablespoon minced garlic

4 teaspoons extra-virgin olive oil

1 Place the beans in a large pot with water to cover. Turn the heat to high and bring to a boil.

2 Cut a slit in the onion and insert the bay leaf; insert the clove into the onion as well and put the onion in the pot. Turn the heat down so the beans simmer. Cover loosely.

3 When the beans begin to soften, after about 30 minutes, season with salt and pepper. Continue to cook, stirring occasionally, until the beans are tender but still intact, about 1 hour; add additional water if necessary.

4 Add the greens to the pot and continue to cook until they are tender, 10 to 30 minutes, depending on the thickness of the stems. If you want a soupy mixture, add more water.

5 Remove the onion. Season the stew with additional salt and pepper. About 3 minutes before serving, add the garlic and stir. Spoon the beans and greens into individual bowls and drizzle with olive oil (or see the variation, below). Serve immediately.

Ⓥ Beans and Greens Gratin Cook as above. When you're done, stir in 1 table-spoon olive oil and spread the mixture in a lightly oiled baking dish. Preheat the broiler. Top the mixture with 1 cup bread crumbs . Drizzle with more olive oil to taste. Run under the broiler, about 4 to 6 inches from the heat source, until lightly browned, about 5 minutes. Serve hot or at room temperature.

Sautéed Beans and Tomatoes

An elegant side dish which is even better if you use Vegetable Stock (page XXX) to cook the dried beans.

Makes 4 servings

Time: 20 minutes with precooked beans

2 tablespoons butter (preferred) or extra-virgin olive oil

1 tablespoon minced shallot or scallion

1 teaspoon fresh thyme leaves or ½ teaspoon dried thyme

2 cups peeled, seeded, and diced tomatoes (canned are fine; drain them first)

4 cups drained cooked or canned white beans

½ cup Vegetable Stock (page 29), store-bought vegetable broth, juice from canned tomatoes, or water

Salt and freshly ground black pepper to taste

1 Place the butter or oil in a large, deep skillet and turn the heat to medium. A minute later, add the shallot and cook, stirring, until it softens, 3 to 5 minutes. Add the thyme and cook for about 30 seconds.

2 Add the tomatoes and cook, stirring occasionally, until they break up and become "saucy," about 10 minutes. Then add the beans and stock and turn the heat to medium-high. Cook, stirring, until the mixture is hot and creamy, about 5 minutes. Season and serve.

Black Beans with Cumin or Chili

Earthy, full-flavored black beans are at their best when highly seasoned. Remember that older black beans can take forever to cook (or so it seems).

Makes 4 to 8 servings

Time: 1½ to 2 hours, largely unattended

1 pound black beans, washed and picked over (see Tips, page 73)

2 bay leaves

4 cloves garlic

2 tablespoons ground cumin or chili powder

A few sprigs thyme or ½ teaspoon dried thyme

Salt and freshly ground black pepper to taste

1 medium onion, minced

1. Place the beans in a large pot with water to cover. Turn the heat to high and bring to a boil.

2. Add the bay leaves; crush and peel 2 garlic cloves and add them too. Add the cumin or chili powder and thyme. Turn the heat down so the beans simmer and cover loosely.

3. When the beans begin to soften, season with salt and pepper. Continue to cook, stirring occasionally, until the beans are very tender, at least 1 hour; add additional water if necessary.

4. Mince the remaining garlic and add it to the pot along with the onion. Cook 5 to 10 minutes longer and season with additional salt, pepper, and cumin or chili powder. Remove and discard the bay leaves. Serve with rice.

Red Beans and Rice

This combination of rice, beans, and coconut milk is a staple throughout the Caribbean, a cross-cultural marvel that makes a satisfying and delicious main course.

Makes 4 to 6 servings

Time: About 30 minutes with precooked beans

3 cups Red Beans (at right)

1½ cups long-grain rice

3 cups canned or Fresh Coconut Milk (at right), warmed

Salt and freshly ground black pepper to taste

Minced fresh parsley leaves for garnish

1 Place the beans in a saucepan that can hold at least double their bulk comfortably. Turn the heat to medium-low and warm gently. If there is a great deal of liquid in the beans, cook them, stirring frequently, until they are moist but not swimming in liquid.

2 Add the rice and the coconut milk to the beans. Cover and turn the heat to low. Cook for about 20 minutes, or until the rice is tender and the liquid is absorbed. If necessary, uncover and raise the heat to medium-high; cook, stirring, until the liquid is absorbed. Season with salt and pepper, garnish, and serve.

Ⓥ Red Beans

Makes 6 to 8 servings • Time: About 2 hours, largely unattended

Essentially a vegetable stew with beans (or a bean stew with vegetables), this can be varied according to what you have on hand. Some people will like it with a little heat added (in the form of a couple of dried chiles); others might like a touch of sugar.

2 cups kidney, pinto, or other beans, washed and picked over

2 tablespoons olive oil

2 large onions, chopped

2 bell peppers, stemmed, seeded, and chopped

2 celery stalks, chopped

1 tablespoon minced garlic

4 or 5 sprigs thyme or 1 teaspoon dried thyme

2 bay leaves

¼ teaspoon ground allspice

2 cups chopped tomatoes (canned are fine; don't drain)

Salt and freshly ground black pepper to taste

Minced fresh parsley or cilantro leaves for garnish

Tabasco sauce (optional)

1 Place the beans in a large pot with water to cover. Turn the heat to high and bring to a boil; skim the foam if necessary. Turn the heat down so the beans simmer. Cover loosely and stir very occasionally; add additional water if necessary.

2 Place the oil in a large skillet over medium heat. When the oil shimmers cook the onion, pepper, celery, and garlic in the oil, stirring frequently, until the pepper is softened, about 10 minutes. Add the thyme, bay leaves, allspice, and tomatoes.

Turn the heat to medium-low and cook, stirring, until the tomatoes break up, 10 to 15 minutes.

3 Pour the vegetable mixture into the pot with the beans. Cook, until the beans are very tender, about an hour or more. Remove and discard the bay leaves. Taste and add salt and pepper if necessary. Garnish and serve, passing Tabasco or other hot sauce at the table.

Ⓥ Fresh Coconut Milk

Makes about 2 cups • Time: 20 minutes

You can buy coconut milk in cans, but it's relatively expensive and, for me at least, more trouble than it's worth. On the other hand, a pound of dried coconut costs about $2 at the natural foods store and will make gallons of coconut milk, thick or thin, with little effort. Be careful when blending this—it's hot.

2 cups water, plus 1 to 2 cups more if needed

2 cups dried unsweetened shredded or grated coconut

1 Bring 2 cups of water to a boil. Put the coconut in the container of a blender.

2 Pour 2 cups of water into the blender. Use a towel to hold the lid on tight and turn the switch on and off a few times quickly to get the mixture going. Then blend for about 30 seconds. Let rest for 10 minutes.

3 Pour the milk through a strainer. This will be fairly thick. If you need more milk, just pour additional water through the coconut, up to another cup or two. Press the coconut to extract as much liquid as possible. Use immediately or freeze indefinitely.

Lentils and Rice with Caramelized Onions

This Middle Eastern staple is one of my favorite lunch dishes, a vegetarian one-pot meal that is easy, highly seasoned, and a nice break from sandwiches and pasta. Omit the caramelized onions if you like, but you should try them at least once; they are a sensational garnish.

Makes 4 servings

Time: About 45 minutes

3 tablespoons olive oil

1 medium onion, chopped, plus 1 large or 2 medium onions, halved and sliced

1 teaspoon minced garlic

1 teaspoon ground cumin

Salt and freshly ground black pepper to taste

2 cups lentils, washed and picked over (see Tips, page 73)

About 6 cups Vegetable Stock (page 29), store-bought vegetable broth, or water, warmed

1 cup long- or short-grain rice

Minced fresh parsley leaves for garnish

1 Place 1 tablespoon of the oil in a large, deep saucepan and turn the heat to medium. A minute later, add the chopped onion and cook until it begins to become tender, about 5 minutes. Add the garlic, cumin, salt, and pepper, and cook 3 minutes more. Add the lentils, stir, and add about 4 cups liquid.

2 Cook, stirring occasionally, until the lentils begin to soften, about 20 minutes. Add enough of the remaining stock or water so that the lentils are covered by about an inch of liquid. Stir in the rice. Cover and turn the heat to low.

3 Meanwhile, place the remaining oil in a medium skillet and turn the heat to medium-high. Cook the onion slices, stirring frequently, until they are dark brown but not burned, about 15 minutes. Scoop out the onions and let them drain on paper towels while you finish cooking the lentils and rice.

4 Check the rice and lentils after 20 minutes. When both are tender and the liquid is absorbed, the dish is ready. If the lentils and rice are not tender, add more liquid, cover, and cook for a few more minutes. If, on the contrary, the rice and lentils are soft and there is much liquid remaining, raise the heat a bit and cook, uncovered, stirring, until it evaporates.

5 Serve the rice and lentils, garnished with the caramelized onions and parsley.

Ⓥ Baked Beans

These are fairly simple baked beans, traditional, and meatless. This doesn't mean they are limited, however; see 4 Vegetarian Ideas for Baked Beans, below.

Makes 4 servings

Time: At least 4 hours, largely unattended

1 pound navy, pea, or other white beans

2 tablespoons butter or neutral oil like corn or canola

1 large or 2 medium onions, quartered

2 cups peeled, seeded, and chopped tomatoes (canned are fine; don't bother to drain)

½ cup molasses, or to taste

2 teaspoons ground mustard or 2 tablespoons prepared mustard, or to taste

Salt and freshly ground black pepper to taste

1 Cook the beans as in Basic Beans (page 72), but only until they begin to become tender, about 30 minutes.

2 Preheat the oven to 300°F. Put the butter or oil and the onions in the bottom of a bean pot or other deep-sided ovenproof covered pot, such as a Dutch oven. Drain the beans, then mix them with the tomatoes, molasses, and mustard. Pour them over the onions. Gently add enough boiling water to cover the beans by about an inch.

3 Bake, uncovered, for about 3 hours, checking occasionally and adding more water if necessary. At the end of 3 hours, add salt and pepper to taste; you may also add more molasses, or mustard. Serve hot.

4 Vegetarian Ideas for Baked Beans

1 Add ketchup (essentially another sweetener, since it is mostly corn syrup) to taste or substitute sugar or maple syrup (or a combination) for the molasses.

2 Add Worcestershire, soy, or Tabasco sauce to taste.

3 Add a few chunks of peeled carrots.

4 Use pinto, kidney, or lima beans.

ⓥ Chili non Carne

Chili can be quite simple, or more complicated. Although some chili purists insist that chili should be made with meat and no beans, I like bean-based chili. All chili contains chili powder or, even more basic, a combination of ground chiles, cumin, and oregano.

Makes 4 servings

Time: About 2 hours, largely unattended

2 cups pinto, kidney, or other beans, washed and picked over (see Tips, page 73)

1 whole onion, unpeeled, plus 1 small onion, minced

Salt and freshly ground black pepper to taste

1 cup bean cooking liquid, Vegetable Stock (page 29), store-bought vegetable broth, or water

1 fresh or dried hot chile, seeded, stemmed, and minced, or to taste (optional)

1 teaspoon ground cumin, or to taste (optional)

1 teaspoon minced fresh oregano leaves or 1/2 teaspoon dried oregano (optional)

1 tablespoon chili powder (optional), if you prefer it to the combination of pepper, cumin, and oregano above

1 tablespoon minced garlic

Minced cilantro leaves for garnish

1 Place the beans in a large pot with water to cover. Turn the heat to high and bring to a boil; skim the foam if necessary. Add the whole onion. Turn the heat down so the beans simmer and cover loosely.

2 When the beans begin to soften, season with salt and pepper. Continue to cook, stirring occasionally, until the beans are quite tender but still intact, 1 to 2 hours; add additional water if necessary.

3 Drain the beans, reserving the cooking liquid if you choose to use it. Discard the onion and add all the remaining ingredients except cilantro. Turn the heat to medium and bring to a boil. Cover and turn the heat to low.

4 Cook, stirring occasionally and adding more liquid if necessary, until the beans are very tender and the flavors have mellowed, about 15 minutes. Adjust seasoning as necessary and garnish with cilantro. Serve with rice, crackers, or tortilla chips, and bottled hot sauce, such as Tabasco.

ⓥ **Chili with Tomatoes** Substitute 2 cups peeled, seeded, and chopped tomatoes (canned are fine; don't bother to drain) for the bean or other liquid. Add 1/4 teaspoon ground cinnamon with the other spices. Cook carefully, adding a little bit more liquid if needed. For a non-vegan addition, top with freshly grated Cheddar or jack cheese if you like.

Simple Bean Croquettes

The most basic of all bean cakes. Vary the seasoning as you like, substituting cilantro for parsley, or adding a bit of garlic, cayenne, cumin, or chile powder.

Makes 4 servings

Time: 20 minutes with precooked beans

2 cups drained cooked or canned white or other beans, with a few tablespoons bean cooking liquid reserved (see Step 1)

1/2 cup minced onion

1/4 cup minced fresh parsley leaves

1 egg, lightly beaten

Salt and freshly ground black pepper to taste

About 1/2 cup coarse cornmeal or bread crumbs

Peanut or other oil as needed

3 Simple Ways to Use Bean Croquettes

1 Use as a veggie burger: Place on a roll with lettuce, tomato, and dressing.

2 Use as a breakfast side dish in place of potatoes or meat.

3 Use as a main course at dinner, with any sauce you like, such as Pesto (page 48) or Tomato-Onion Salsa (page 7).

1 If you want to serve the croquettes hot, preheat the oven to 200°F. Mash the beans by putting them through a food mill or into a blender or food processor. Use a little bean cooking liquid (or other liquid, such as water or stock) if the beans are too dry to mash. Do not puree; it's nice to leave a few bean chunks in this mixture.

2 Combine the beans with the onion, parsley, egg, salt, and pepper. Add cornmeal or bread crumbs by the tablespoon until you've made a batter that is barely stiff enough to handle. You want to be able to shape it with your hands without it sticking, but it should be quite fragile or the cakes will be dry.

3 Cover the bottom of a large, deep skillet with about 1/8 inch of oil; turn the heat to medium. Shape 1/4 of the bean mixture into a hamburger-shaped cake and place in the skillet. Repeat with the remaining batter.

4 Cook the croquettes until nicely browned on both sides, adjusting the heat so that they brown evenly without burning before turning, 3 to 5 minutes per side. Keep warm in the oven until ready to serve—for up to 30 minutes—or serve at room temperature.

Bean Croquettes with Southwestern Flavors Substitute cilantro for the parsley. Add to the mix: 1/2 teaspoon minced garlic; 1 jalapeño or other fresh hot or dried pepper, stemmed, seeded, and minced; 1 teaspoon ground cumin; 1 tablespoon tomato paste; 1/4 cup minced red or yellow bell pepper; and 1 tablespoon freshly squeezed lime juice. Make sure to add enough cornmeal (better than bread crumbs, in this case) to the mix to compensate for the added liquids.

Split Peas, Mung Beans, or Lentils with Curry

Red lentils and split peas—part of the large group of legumes called *dal* in India—become soft quickly, so the cooking time here is minimal. It's a wonderful winter side dish—or even a main course, with rice—when good fresh vegetables are scarce. Although this basic recipe is fine, the more interesting variation doesn't take much longer.

Makes 4 servings

Time: 30 minutes to 1 hour

1½ cups yellow (preferred) or green split peas, or yellow mung beans, or red lentils, washed and picked over (see Tips, page 73)

4 cups Vegetable Stock (page 29), store-bought vegetable broth, or water, plus more if needed

1 tablespoon curry powder

Salt and freshly ground black pepper to taste

Minced cilantro leaves for garnish

1 Combine the peas, mung beans, or lentils, liquid, curry powder, salt, and pepper in a medium saucepan and bring to a boil over medium-high heat. Turn the heat to medium-low, cover partially, and cook gently, stirring occasionally, until the split peas, mung beans, or lentils are soft and beginning to turn to mush, at least 30 minutes; add additional liquid if necessary. The mixture should be moist but not soupy.

2 Taste and adjust seasoning if necessary. Serve over white rice (preferably basmati), and garnish.

Split Peas, Mung Beans, or Lentils with Mixed Spices Omit the curry powder. Add to the mix: ¼ teaspoon cayenne, or to taste; 1 pinch ground cloves; 1 pinch ground cinnamon; ¼ teaspoon ground cardamom; ½ teaspoon ground coriander; ½ teaspoon ground cumin; ½ teaspoon freshly ground black pepper. Cook as above. When the peas or lentils are nearly done, heat 2 tablespoons butter or peanut (or other) oil in a small skillet over medium-low heat. Add 1 tablespoon each minced garlic and ginger and cook, stirring occasionally, until they soften, 5 to 8 minutes. Stir this mixture into the peas or lentils, garnish with minced cilantro, and serve.

Stir-Fried Tofu with Scallions

You can eat tofu, a mild-tasting, cheese-like substance made from soybeans, simply dressed with soy sauce. Or cut it up and add it to soups, or puree it and use it as a no-cholesterol addition to sauces and salad dressings. When you press tofu, it becomes firmer, easier to manage, and chewier, a combination that pleases everyone. This is a quick and simple stir-fry, one that can be easily varied. Serve with white rice.

Makes 4 servings

Time: 20 minutes

---

1 pound firm or extra-firm tofu, cut into 1-inch cubes

2 tablespoons peanut (preferred) or other oil

1 cup cut-up scallions, cut into 1-inch pieces, the darkest green parts minced and reserved for garnish

½ cup Vegetable Stock (page 29), store-bought vegetable broth, or water

2 tablespoons soy sauce

Salt and freshly ground black pepper to taste

1 Place the tofu on paper towels to drain while you prepare the other ingredients. Let it sit for up to 1 hour or press the tofu (see Tips).

2 Place the oil in a wok or large, deep skillet, preferably non-stick, and turn the heat to medium-high. A minute later, add the scallions; cook, stirring, until they soften, a minute or two.

3 Add the tofu and turn the heat to medium. Cook, stirring only occasionally, until the tofu is heated through. Add the stock and cook until it is reduced by about half, a minute or so, then add the soy sauce and turn off the heat. Taste and add salt and pepper if you like. Garnish with the reserved minced scallions and serve.

Shopping Tip: Tofu is sold in four textures; these are relative rather than absolute terms, but worth noting: Silken: Best for soups, to puree for use in sauces, or to fry; Soft: As soft as silken but also can be pressed, frozen, or marinated and cooked on its own; Firm: Good for stir-fries; can be marinated, pressed, or frozen; Extra-firm: Best for stir-fries.

Preparation Tips: Even though most tofu is packaged (in a small tub filled with water, then wrapped in plastic), it's best to use it as soon as you buy it. If you don't use it all at once, place the remainder in a plastic or glass container, cover it with fresh water, and seal tightly. Change the water daily.

To press tofu (to make it firmer): Cut a brick of tofu in half through its equator. Place each half on a cutting board and prop the board up so that its lower end is at the edge of a sink. Top with another cutting board or similar flat, clean object. Weight the top board with a skillet, a couple of books, whatever. Let sit for 30 to 60 minutes, then drain on paper towels.

Ⓥ Stir-Fried Tofu with Vegetables Steam or parboil 1 cup broccoli or cauliflower florets; they should still be firm, but not crunchy. Substitute them for (or add them to) the scallions in Step 2, cooking until they begin to brown. Proceed as above.

7 | Vegetables

V Vegan

Braised Artichokes with Tarragon

No precooking necessary; just clean the artichokes, cook them in hot oil for a few minutes, then finish with liquid. Substitute any herb you like for the tarragon (chervil is especially nice), or use chopped tomatoes in place of the stock.

Makes 4 servings

Time: 30 minutes

4 large or 12 very small artichokes

3 tablespoons olive oil

1 tablespoon minced garlic

1 tablespoon minced fresh tarragon leaves or 1 teaspoon dried tarragon

1 cup Vegetable Stock (page 29), store-bought vegetable broth, or water

Salt and freshly ground black pepper to taste

1 tablespoon freshly squeezed lemon juice

Minced fresh parsley leaves for garnish

1   If you are using large artichokes, cut them into halves or quarters; remove the leaves and the choke, and trim the bottom. If the artichokes are very small, simply peel off all the leaves and trim the bottom; you can ignore the choke.

2   Heat the oil and garlic together in a large, deep skillet over medium heat, just until the garlic begins to color, about 5 minutes. Add the artichokes and cook, stirring occasionally, for about 5 minutes. Add the tarragon and stock or water, bring to a boil, and cover; turn the heat to medium-low. Cook for about 10 minutes, then turn the artichokes. Check for tenderness every 5 minutes or so; total cooking time will be 15 to 30 minutes.

3   When the artichokes are tender, season with salt and pepper. If there is too much liquid, raise the heat to high for a few minutes and reduce it a bit.

4   Just before serving, sprinkle with lemon juice and garnish.

Trimming Artichokes

   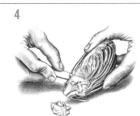

(Step 1) Use scissors or a sharp knife to cut the pointed tips from the tops of an artichoke. (Step 2) Cut the artichoke in half. (Step 3) If desired, cut the artichoke into quarters. (Step 4) Scrape the fuzzy choke out from each of the quarters.

Roasted, Broiled, or Grilled Asparagus

If you're grilling or roasting meat or fish, it's easy to cook the asparagus the same way. And they're great when browned.

Makes 4 servings

Time: 15 minutes, plus preheating time

1½ to 2 pounds asparagus, trimmed and peeled

1 to 2 tablespoons extra-virgin olive oil

Salt to taste

Lemon wedges

1 Preheat the oven to 450°F, preheat the broiler or a gas grill, or start a charcoal or wood fire. If you're roasting or broiling, place the asparagus in a roasting pan and drizzle with a tablespoon or two of oil; sprinkle with salt. If you're grilling, brush the asparagus with oil and sprinkle with salt. Place the asparagus in the oven, under the broiler, or on the grill.

2 Roast or grill, turning the spears once or twice, just until the thick part of the stalks can be pierced with a knife, 10 to 15 minutes. Broiling time will be shorter, 5 to 10 minutes total. Serve immediately, with lemon wedges.

Shopping Tip: Asparagus size is a matter of debate; some people prefer super-thin stalks, which need not be peeled, a distinct advantage. But big, fat stalks are great to eat, too. My recommendation: Take what you get. Don't buy shriveled spears, or damaged ones; and don't buy canned or frozen asparagus.

Preparation Tip: Store asparagus, wrapped loosely in plastic, in the refrigerator. Use as soon as possible.

Preparing Asparagus

Snap off the bottom of each stalk; they will usually separate naturally right where the woody part ends.

All but the thinnest asparagus are best when peeled.

Beet Roesti with Rosemary

An almost unbelievably sweet and wonderful side dish. The sugar in the beets caramelizes, and the flavors of the rosemary, beets, and butter meld beautifully. With thanks to Michael Romano, the brilliant chef at New York's Union Square Café, who shared this recipe with me.

Makes 4 servings

Time: 20 minutes

1 to 1½ pounds beets

1 teaspoon coarsely chopped fresh rosemary

1 teaspoon salt

¼ cup flour

2 tablespoons butter

1 Trim the beets and peel them as you would potatoes; grate them in a food processor or by hand. Begin preheating a medium to large non-stick skillet over medium heat.

2 Toss the grated beets in a bowl with the rosemary and salt, then add about half the flour; toss well, add the rest of the flour, then toss again.

3 Place the butter in the skillet and heat until it begins to turn nut-brown. Scrape the beet mixture into the skillet, shape it into a nice circle, and press it down with a spatula. Turn the heat to medium-high and cook, shaking the pan occasionally, until the bottom of the beet cake is nicely crisp, 6 to 8 minutes. Slide the cake out onto a plate, top with another plate, invert the 2 plates, and slide the cake back into the pan. Continue to cook, adjusting the heat if necessary, until the second side is browned. Cut into wedges and serve immediately.

Shopping Tip: Beets grow spring through fall, but are available pretty much year-round. Size doesn't matter—large beets are easier to handle, and only rarely become woody. Don't buy them if they're mushy. One good indication of freshness is the presence of greens.

Preparation Tips: To store, remove all but an inch of the greens (use them immediately), and place the roots in a plastic bag in the refrigerator. They keep for weeks.

Scrub well before cooking, but leave an inch or so of the green tops on to minimize bleeding.

Cooking Tip: When you can easily pierce a beet with a skewer or thin-bladed knife, it's done. Slight overcooking is usually preferable to undercooking.

Ⓥ Stir-Fried Broccoli

You need not precook the broccoli for these stir-fries, but if you have leftover or extra simmered or steamed broccoli, by all means use them. Just keep the cooking time to a minimum, no longer than it takes to heat the broccoli through.

Makes 4 servings

Time: 30 minutes

About 1½ pounds broccoli, trimmed (page 31)

2 tablespoons peanut (preferred) or other oil

Salt to taste

1 teaspoon sugar

1 cup Vegetable Stock (page 29), store-bought vegetable broth, or water

1 Cut the stalks of the broccoli into thin slices. Separate the florets into small sections.

2 Place the oil in a wok or large, deep skillet over medium-high heat. Two or three minutes later, add the broccoli, raise the heat to high and cook, stirring, until it becomes bright green and glossy and begins to brown, about 5 minutes.

3 Add the salt, sugar, and stock or water. Stir and continue to cook until almost all of the liquid evaporates and the broccoli is tender, about 5 minutes more. Serve immediately.

Ⓥ **Stir-Fried Broccoli with Chinese Mushrooms** In Step 1, soak about ¼ cup dried shiitake ("black") mushrooms in 1 cup hot water until tender; drain them (reserving liquid), trim them, and cut them up. In Step 2, add the mushrooms along with the broccoli. In Step 3, add 1 teaspoon minced garlic and 1 teaspoon peeled and minced fresh ginger along with the salt and sugar. Stir for 15 seconds before adding the strained mushroom soaking liquid and 1 tablespoon of soy sauce.

Cabbage Braised with Onions

Slow-cooked onions add sweetness to this dish, and the touch of cayenne makes it wonderfully spicy. If you use the oil, not the butter, this will be a vegan dish.

Makes 4 servings

Time: About 1 hour

2 cups sliced onions

3 tablespoons butter or olive oil

3 tablespoons tomato paste

¼ teaspoon cayenne, or to taste

½ cup water

1½ to 2 pounds savoy or other white cabbage, cored and shredded (see below)

Salt and freshly ground black pepper to taste

1 Place the onions in a large, deep skillet or casserole over medium-low heat. Cover and cook, stirring every 5 minutes, until the onions have given up their liquid and are almost sticking to the pan. Add the butter or oil, raise the heat to medium-high, and cook for 5 to 10 minutes, until the onion browns nicely.

2 Add the tomato paste, cayenne, water, and cabbage. Stir, then cover. Cook for about 30 minutes, stirring occasionally, until the cabbage is tender but not mushy. Season with salt and pepper and serve.

Coring and Shredding Cabbage

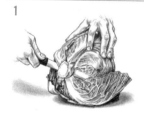 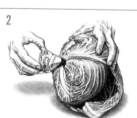  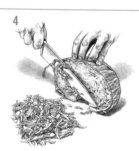

(Steps 1–2) The easiest way to core a head cabbage is to cut a small cone-shaped section from the bottom, then remove it. (Step 3) To shred head cabbage, first cut it into manageable pieces. (Step 4) Cut thin sections across the head; they'll naturally fall into shreds. If the shreds are too long, just cut across them.

Corn-Stuffed Peppers with Spicy Tomato Sauce

Use leftover grains for this dish if you can, but use fresh corn if possible.

Makes 4 servings

Time: About 1 hour

1½ cups cooked white or brown rice, barley, or quinoa

1 medium onion, minced

½ cup diced fresh mushrooms

2 cups cored, peeled, seeded, and diced tomatoes (canned are fine; drain them first)

1½ cups corn kernels, preferably fresh

1 egg, lightly beaten

Salt and freshly ground black pepper to taste

4 red or yellow peppers, caps removed and center hollowed out (page 5)

2 tablespoons peanut or olive oil

2 cloves garlic, crushed

2 small dried hot red chiles

1 tablespoon cumin (seeds or ground)

1 tablespoon soy or Worcestershire sauce, or to taste

2 teaspoons sugar, or to taste

Dry white wine, if needed

Minced fresh chives or parsley leaves for garnish

1 Preheat the oven to 375°F. Combine the grain, onion, mushrooms, half the tomatoes, corn, egg, salt, and pepper. Pack this mixture into the peppers. Place the peppers in a roasting pan with ½ inch of water and bake for 45 minutes, or until the peppers are tender.

2 Meanwhile, make the sauce: Place the oil in a large, deep skillet over medium-high heat. Add the garlic and red chiles and cook, stirring, until the garlic is golden; scoop out the garlic and chiles and discard. Add the cumin and stir. Add the remaining tomatoes, crushing them with a fork or spoon. Bring to a boil, turn the heat to medium-low, and add the soy sauce. Simmer gently for 10 minutes, then taste and add sugar as necessary; season with salt and pepper. Thin with a little wine if necessary. Puree in a blender and keep warm.

3 Serve the peppers with a little of the sauce spooned over, garnished with chives or parsley. Pass the remaining sauce at the table.

Eggplant Parmesan

To save both time and effort, you can use broiled eggplant slices (at right) in this dish, omitting the sautéing of the eggplant. In Parma (where we must suppose this dish originated), no one would dream of using mozzarella here, and you should try it that way at least once.

Makes 6 servings

Time: About 1 hour, longer if you choose to salt the eggplant

---

2 medium-to-large eggplant (2 to 3 pounds total)

Salt (optional)

Olive oil as needed

Flour for dredging

Freshly ground black pepper to taste

2 cups tomato sauce (from Pasta with Basic Tomato Sauce, page 42)

1/2 pound grated mozzarella cheese, about 2 cups (optional)

1 cup freshly grated Parmesan cheese, plus more if you omit the mozzarella

About 30 fresh basil leaves

1 Peel the eggplant if the skin is thick or the eggplant is less than perfectly firm. Cut it into 1/2-inch-thick slices and salt it if you like (see below).

2 When you're ready to cook, preheat the oven to 350°F. Place about 3 tablespoons of olive oil in a large skillet and turn the heat to medium. When the oil is hot (a pinch of flour will sizzle), dredge the eggplant slices, one at a time, in the flour, shaking off the excess. Place in the pan, but do not crowd; you will have to cook in batches. Cook for 3 or 4 minutes on each side, until nicely browned, then drain on paper towels. Add some pepper to the slices as they cook, as well as some salt if you did not salt the eggplant. Add more oil to the skillet as needed.

3 Lightly oil a baking dish, then spoon about 1/2 of the tomato sauce into it. Top with a layer of eggplant, then a thin layer of each of the cheeses, and finally a few basil leaves. Repeat until all the ingredients are used up, reserving some of the basil for garnish. End with a sprinkling of Parmesan.

4 Bake for 20 to 30 minutes, or until the dish is bubbling hot. Mince the remaining basil and sprinkle over the top. Serve hot or at room temperature.

Preparation Tips: Eggplant need not be peeled unless the skin is very thick, or, of course, unless you prefer to do so.

It's usually worth salting larger eggplant, a process which draws out excess moisture and a certain amount of bitterness along with it. Trim off the ends, then cut it into slices (you can cut long slices or crosswise ones) from 1/2 to 1 inch thick. Or cut it into chunks. Sprinkle both sides of the slices (or all sides of the chunks) liberally with coarse salt, then let drain in a colander for at least half an hour, or up to 2 hours. Rinse and squeeze dry between paper or cloth towels.

Ⓥ Grilled or Broiled Eggplant Slices

Makes 4 servings • Time: 20 minutes, plus time to preheat the grill and salt the eggplant

This is the simplest way to prepare eggplant, and it makes a delicious side dish or can be used in Eggplant Parmesan.

1 medium-to-large eggplant (1 to 1½ pounds)	Salt and freshly ground black pepper to taste
1 teaspoon minced garlic (optional)	Minced fresh parsley leaves for garnish
4 to 6 tablespoons olive oil	

1 Peel the eggplant if the skin is thick or the eggplant is less than perfectly firm. Cut it into ½-inch-thick slices and salt it if you like. Start a charcoal or wood fire or preheat a gas grill or broiler; the rack should be 4 to 6 inches from the heat source.

2 Stir the optional garlic into the olive oil, then brush one side of the eggplant slices with the oil. Place, oiled side down, on a baking sheet or directly on the grill. Sprinkle with salt (if you salted the eggplant, hold off) and pepper, then brush with more oil.

3 Broil or grill until browned on both sides, turning once or twice and brushing with more oil if the eggplant looks dry. Serve hot or at room temperature, garnished with parsley.

Grilled Portobello Mushrooms

You can grill just the caps of portobellos if you like, or cut them down the middle and grill cap and stem together; make sure the stem is washed well.

Makes 4 servings

Time: About 20 minutes, plus time to preheat the grill

⅓ cup extra-virgin olive oil

1 tablespoon minced shallot, scallion, or onion

Salt and freshly ground black pepper to taste

4 large portobello mushrooms, trimmed and cut in half right down the middle

Minced fresh parsley or chervil leaves for garnish

1 Start a charcoal or wood fire or preheat a gas grill or broiler; the fire should be quite hot and the rack about 4 inches from the heat source. Mix together the olive oil, shallot, salt, and pepper and brush the mushrooms all over with about half of this mixture.

2 Grill or broil the mushrooms with the tops of their caps away from the heat until they begin to brown, 5 to 8 minutes. Brush with the remaining oil and turn. Grill until tender and nicely browned all over, 5 to 10 minutes more. Garnish and serve.

Preparation Tip: To trim mushrooms, cut off any hard or dried-out spots—usually just the end of the stem. The stems of most mushrooms are perfectly edible (those of shiitakes are not, but they can be used for stock). Rinse off any dirt in running water, but quickly, or the mushrooms may become waterlogged.

Potato Pancakes

These are the traditional latkes, served in many Jewish households during Hanukkah, but they are delicious any time of year, with applesauce or sour cream.

Makes 6 servings

Time: About 40 minutes

About 2 pounds baking potatoes, such as Idaho or Russet, peeled

1 medium onion

2 eggs

Salt and freshly ground black pepper to taste

2 tablespoons plain bread crumbs or matzo meal

Canola or other neutral oil as needed

1 Grate the potatoes by hand or with the grating disk of a food processor. Drain in a colander or strainer; grate the onion. Preheat the oven to 200°F.

2 In a large bowl, beat the eggs with the salt, pepper, and bread crumbs or matzo meal; stir in the potatoes and onion.

3 Place a ⅛-inch layer of oil in a large, deep skillet and turn the heat to medium. When the oil is hot, drop the potato batter into it by the quarter-cup or large spoon. Cook until browned on both sides, about 10 minutes per pancake. Drain pancakes on paper towels and keep warm in the oven until all of them are finished. Serve hot.

V Sesame Spinach

This is the cold spinach dish served in many Japanese restaurants. If you want basic cooked spinach, simply cook the spinach as below, dressing it with oil or butter before serving.

Makes 4 servings

Time: 20 minutes

½ cup sesame seeds

10 ounces spinach, cleaned, tough stems removed

Salt to taste

1 teaspoon soy sauce

1 teaspoon dark sesame oil

1 Bring a large pot of water to boil, and add salt. While you are waiting, toast the sesame seeds by heating them in a dry skillet over medium heat, shaking occasionally, until they begin to pop and color; place them in a small bowl.

2 When the water boils, cook the spinach until it wilts and the stems become tender, 30 seconds to 2 minutes. Remove it with a strainer or slotted spoon and immediately plunge it into a bowl of ice water; when it has cooled off, squeeze the excess water from it and chop it fine.

3 Sprinkle the spinach with a little salt and the soy sauce and shape it into a 1-inch-thick log (if you have a bamboo sushi-rolling mat, use this to achieve a perfect shape). Cut the log into 1-inch-long slices; dip each end of each slice into the sesame seeds and arrange on a plate. Drizzle with the sesame oil. Serve immediately or refrigerate.

Sautéed Summer Squash or Zucchini

Salting grated summer squash enables you to brown it quickly, but it isn't essential.

Makes 4 servings

Time: 15 to 45 minutes

About 2 pounds summer squash
or zucchini, the smaller the better

1 tablespoon salt (optional)

3 to 4 tablespoons olive or other oil

1 clove garlic, smashed (optional)

Freshly ground black pepper to taste

Minced fresh mint, parsley, or basil
leaves for garnish

1 Coarsely grate the squash by hand or with the grating disk of a food processor. If time allows, place grated squash in a colander and salt it liberally—use 1 tablespoon or more of salt. Toss to blend and let drain for at least 30 minutes. Rinse quickly and dry by wringing in a towel.

2 When you're ready to cook, place the oil in a large non-stick skillet and turn the heat to medium-high; add the garlic if you choose to do so. When the oil is hot, toss the squash in the oil, sprinkle with pepper, and raise the heat to high. Cook, stirring frequently, until the squash is browned, about 10 minutes. Garnish and serve hot.

Braised Butternut or Other Winter Squash with Garlic

One of those dishes whose wonderful flavor belies its simplicity. Great served with Grilled Portobello Mushrooms, page 96.

Makes 4 servings

Time: About 30 minutes

2 tablespoons olive oil

1 tablespoon minced garlic

1½ pounds butternut or other winter squash, peeled and cut into ½- to 1-inch cubes

¼ cup Vegetable Stock (page 29), store-bought vegetable broth, or water

Salt and freshly ground black pepper to taste

Minced fresh parsley leaves for garnish

1 Place the olive oil and garlic in a large, deep skillet and turn the heat to medium. When the garlic begins to color, add the squash, stock or water, salt, and pepper. Bring to a boil, cover, and turn the heat to low. Cook, stirring once or twice, until the squash is tender, about 15 minutes.

2 Uncover the pan and turn the heat to medium-high. Cook, shaking the pan occasionally and stirring somewhat less often, until all the liquid is evaporated and the squash has begun to brown, 5 to 10 minutes. Turn the heat to low and cook until the squash is as browned and crisp as you like.

3 Taste and adjust seasoning, garnish, and serve.

Preparation Tip: To prepare hard-skinned squashes, use a cleaver or very large knife to split the squash in half. Scoop out the seeds and strings and discard (or bake the seeds as you would Fiery Pumpkin Seeds, page 33). Peeling butternut squash is fairly easy, as long as you have a sturdy vegetable peeler or a paring knife. Peeling acorn and other odd-shaped squash is virtually impossible, so don't try.

Grilled Mixed Vegetables

This is a "for instance" recipe. You can grill almost any vegetable, as long as you cut it into thicker slices—no less than 1/2 inch thick—so they don't fall apart. Soft vegetables, such as zucchini, can be cut even thicker.

Very hard vegetables, such as potatoes (always use waxy red or white potatoes for grilling), are best parboiled until nearly tender before grilling.

Makes 4 to 6 servings

Time: 45 minutes, plus time to preheat the grill

---

1 Spanish or other large onion

2 red or yellow bell peppers, stemmed, halved, and seeded

1 eggplant, cut into 1/2-inch-thick slices and salted (page 94) if time allows

1 zucchini, cut lengthwise into 1/2-inch-thick slices

Extra-virgin olive oil as needed

Salt and freshly ground black pepper to taste

Minced parsley leaves for garnish

1 Start a charcoal or wood fire or preheat a gas grill. Cut the root and flower end from the onion so that it will sit flat on the grill. Then cut it in half, through its equator. Prepare the other vegetables.

2 Brush all the vegetables liberally with olive oil and sprinkle with salt and pepper. Grill, turning once or twice, until nicely browned on both sides and tender throughout, about 15 minutes. Drizzle with a little more olive oil if you like, garnish, and serve hot or at room temperature.

Ⓥ Grilled Vegetables with Garlic Cut one or more whole heads of garlic in half through their equator. Brush with olive oil and grill over a relatively cool part of the grill until the garlic becomes soft. Spoon the meat out from its husk and combine it with the vegetables before serving.

8 | Breads and Desserts

Ⓥ Vegan

Corn Bread

With the possible exception of brownies, there is no other baked good that packs so much flavor, and can be used in so many situations, with so little work. This batter can also be made into muffins or, if you have a mold, corn sticks.

You can make corn bread with sweet milk or buttermilk, yogurt, or soured milk; the major difference is taste, although buttermilk (or soured milk) makes a somewhat lighter bread.

Makes about 6 servings

Time: About 45 minutes

1¼ cups buttermilk, milk, or yogurt (or 1¼ cups milk and 1 tablespoon white vinegar—see Step 2), plus more as needed

2 tablespoons butter or olive oil

1½ cups (about 7 ounces) medium-grind cornmeal

½ cup all-purpose flour

1½ teaspoons baking powder

1 teaspoon salt

1 tablespoon sugar, plus more if you like sweet corn bread

1 egg

5 Vegetarian Additions to Corn Bread

1 Chili powder or cumin, about 1 tablespoon

2 Fresh or creamed corn, about 1 cup

3 Grated cheese, typically Cheddar, about 1 cup

4 Molasses or honey, in place of the sugar, about ¼ cup

5 Minced herbs, especially cilantro or fresh parsley, about 2 tablespoons

1 Preheat the oven to 375°F.

2 If you are using buttermilk, milk, or yogurt, ignore this step. If you want to use soured milk (a good substitute for buttermilk), warm the milk gently—1 minute in the microwave is sufficient, just enough to take the chill off—and add the vinegar. Let it rest while you prepare the other ingredients.

3 Place the fat in a medium ovenproof skillet or in an 8-inch square baking pan over medium heat; heat until good and hot, about 2 minutes, then turn off the heat. Meanwhile, combine the dry ingredients in a bowl. Mix the egg into the buttermilk, milk, yogurt, or soured milk. Stir the liquid mixture into the dry ingredients, combining well; if it seems too dry, add another tablespoon or two of milk. Pour the batter into the preheated fat, smooth out the top if necessary, and place in the oven.

4 Bake about 30 minutes, until the top is lightly browned and the sides have pulled away from the pan; a toothpick inserted into the center will come out clean. Serve hot or warm.

Lighter, Richer Corn Bread Use 4 tablespoons of butter (do not use other fat). Increase sugar to ¼ cup. Use 2 eggs; stir their yolks into the milk, as above, and beat the whites until stiff but not dry, then gently stir them into the prepared batter after yolks and milk have been incorporated. Bake as above.

Corn and Bean Bread Surprisingly wonderful. Use 2 eggs and 1 cup buttermilk or soured milk; omit the white flour. Stir 1½ cups well-cooked white beans (canned are fine), pureed and strained, into the milk-egg mixture before adding to the dry ingredients. Proceed as above.

Nut Bread

This is a good bread for snacks, breakfast, or brunch, and one you can easily vary. Substitute 2 tablespoons canola or other neutral oil for the butter if you would like a bread lower in saturated fat.

Makes 1 loaf

Time: About 1¼ hours

¼ cup melted butter, plus butter for greasing the pan

3 cups (about 14 ounces) all-purpose flour (or use 1½ cups all-purpose and 1½ cups whole wheat)

4 teaspoons baking powder

1 teaspoon salt

½ teaspoon ground cinnamon

⅔ cup sugar

1½ cups milk

1 egg

1 cup roughly chopped walnuts or pecans

1 Preheat the oven to 350°F. Butter a 9 × 5-inch loaf pan.

2 Mix together the flour, baking powder, salt, cinnamon, and sugar. Beat together the milk, melted butter, and egg. Make a well in the center of the dry ingredients and pour the wet ingredients into it. Using a large spoon or rubber spatula, combine the ingredients swiftly, stirring and folding rather than beating, and stopping as soon as all the dry ingredients are moistened. The batter should be lumpy, not smooth.

3 Gently stir in the walnuts, and pour and scrape the batter into the buttered pan. Bake for about 45 minutes to 1 hour, or until a toothpick inserted into the center comes out clean. Cool on a rack for at least 10 minutes before removing from the pan.

Raisin or Nut-and-Raisin Bread Substitute raisins for the nuts, or add raisins in addition to the nuts; the total of nuts and raisins should be no more than 1½ cups. Increase cinnamon to 1 teaspoon and add a pinch of ground cloves.

Date-Nut Bread Reduce the nuts to ½ cup and add 1 cup chopped dates (or prunes, figs, or apricots) to the mix. Use brown sugar in place of regular sugar. Add 1 teaspoon vanilla extract to the wet ingredients.

Basic Muffins

Fast, easy, and almost infinitely variable (there isn't a single quick-bread batter that cannot be baked as muffins, or vice versa), muffins have somehow become the domain of doughnut shops. But baking at home gives you control over fat content and quality of ingredients, and introduces you to one of life's great luxuries: the fresh-from-the-oven muffin. I do not like very sweet muffins, so I have kept the sugar to a minimum, but you can double it with no ill effects if you like.

Makes 8 large or 12 medium muffins

Time: About 40 minutes

3 tablespoons melted butter or canola or other neutral oil, plus some for greasing the muffin tin

2 cups (about 9 ounces) all-purpose flour

1/4 cup sugar, or to taste

1/2 teaspoon salt

3 teaspoons baking powder

1 egg

1 cup milk, plus more if needed

1 Preheat the oven to 400°F. Grease a standard 12-compartment muffin tin.

2 Mix together the dry ingredients in a bowl. Beat together the egg, milk, and melted butter or oil. Make a well in the center of the dry ingredients and pour the wet ingredients into it. Using a large spoon or rubber spatula, combine the ingredients swiftly, stirring and folding rather than beating, and stopping as soon as all the dry ingredients are moistened. The batter should be lumpy, not smooth, and thick but quite moist; add a little more milk or other liquid if necessary.

3 Spoon the batter into the muffin tins, filling them about two-thirds full and handling the batter as little as possible. (If you prefer bigger muffins, fill the cups almost to the top. Pour 1/4 cup water into those cups left empty.) Bake 20 to 30 minutes, or until the muffins are nicely browned and a toothpick inserted into the center of one of them comes out clean. Remove from the oven and let rest for 5 minutes before taking them out of the tin. Serve warm.

Bran Muffins Substitute 1 cup oat or wheat bran for 1 cup of the all-purpose flour (you can use whole wheat flour for the remainder if you like). Use 2 eggs and honey, molasses, or maple syrup in place of the sugar. Add $1/2$ cup raisins to the prepared batter if you like.

Savory Muffins Cut sugar back to 1 tablespoon. Add up to 1 cup of minced or shredded cheese, or a $1/4$ cup each minced onions and red bell peppers to the batter just before baking.

Blueberry or Cranberry Muffins Add 1 teaspoon ground cinnamon to the dry ingredients; increase sugar to $1/2$ cup. Stir 1 cup fresh blueberries or cranberries into the batter at the last minute. You can also use frozen blueberries or cranberries here; do not defrost them first. Blueberry muffins are good with $1/2$ teaspoon lemon zest added to the batter along with the wet ingredients. Cranberry muffins are excellent with $1/2$ cup chopped nuts and/or 1 tablespoon minced orange zest added to the prepared batter.

Coffee Cake Muffins Mix together $1/2$ cup packed brown sugar; 1 teaspoon ground cinnamon; 1 cup finely chopped walnuts, pecans, or cashews; and 2 extra tablespoons melted butter. Stir half of this mixture into the original batter with the wet ingredients, and sprinkle the rest on top before baking.

Pear Clafouti

This traditional French dessert is essentially a large, sweet pancake baked with fruit. It is among the best desserts you can make at the last minute. Put it in the oven when you sit down to dinner and you can eat it for dessert.

Makes 4 to 6 servings

Time: 1 hour

1 tablespoon unsalted butter,
more or less, for greasing the pan

½ cup sugar, plus some for dusting
the pan

About 4 pears, peeled, halved, and cored

3 eggs

⅓ cup all-purpose flour

¾ cup heavy cream or plain yogurt

¾ cup milk

1 teaspoon vanilla extract

Pinch salt

Confectioners' sugar

1 Preheat the oven to 350°F. Butter a gratin dish, about 9 × 5 × 2 inches deep, or a 10-inch round deep pie plate or porcelain dish; sprinkle it with sugar, then invert to remove the excess. Lay the pears in one layer in the dish.

2 Beat the eggs until foamy. Add the ½ cup of sugar and beat with a whisk or electric mixer until foamy and fairly thick.

3 Add the flour and continue to beat until thick and smooth. Add the cream, milk, vanilla, and salt.

4 Pour the batter over the pears. Bake for about 20 minutes, or until the clafouti is nicely browned on top and a knife inserted into it comes out clean. Sift some confectioners' sugar over it and serve warm or at room temperature.

Blueberry Cobbler

I've made this recipe dozens of times, and it's always been a hit. I love it with blueberries, but you can make it with any fruit you like.

Makes 6 to 8 servings

Time: About 1 hour

---

4 to 6 cups blueberries or other fruit, washed and well dried

1 cup sugar, or to taste

8 tablespoons (1 stick) cold unsalted butter, cut into bits, plus some for greasing the pan

½ cup all-purpose flour

½ teaspoon baking powder

Pinch salt

1 egg

½ teaspoon vanilla extract

1 Preheat the oven to 375°F. Toss the fruit with half the sugar, and spread it in a lightly buttered 8-inch square or 9-inch round baking pan.

2 Combine the flour, baking powder, salt, and ½ cup sugar in the container of a food processor and pulse once or twice. Add the butter and process for 10 seconds, until the mixture is well blended. By hand, beat in the egg and vanilla.

3 Drop this mixture onto the fruit by tablespoonfuls; do not spread it out. Bake until golden yellow and just starting to brown, 35 to 45 minutes. Serve immediately.

Angel Food Cake

Light and wonderful, with virtually no fat and a lovely crust whose flavor can't be beat. Serve with any fruit sauces (see Raspberry, Strawberry, or Other Fruit Sauce, at right), Chocolate Sauce (at right), or simply with some sliced fruit tossed with a little sugar.

Makes at least 10 servings

Time: About 1½ hours, plus time to cool

1 cup (about 4½ ounces) cake flour, sifted (do not use all-purpose flour)

1½ cups sugar

9 egg whites

¼ teaspoon salt

1 teaspoon cream of tartar

1 teaspoon vanilla extract

½ teaspoon almond extract

1   Preheat the oven to 325°F.

2   Sift together the flour and ½ cup of the sugar. Repeat.

3   Beat the egg whites until foamy. Add the salt and cream of tartar and continue to beat until they hold soft peaks; the tops of the whites should droop a little bit when you remove the beaters. Beat in the remaining sugar and vanilla and almond extracts and continue to beat until the peaks become a little stiffer.

4   Gradually and gently fold in the flour mixture, using a rubber spatula or your hand. Turn the batter into an ungreased 9- or 10-inch tube pan (not one with ridged sides) and bake 45 minutes to 1 hour, until the cake is firm, resilient, and nicely browned.

5   Invert the cake onto a rack and let cool for about an hour. Cut carefully around the sides of the cake and remove. Cool completely before slicing with a serrated knife or pulling apart with two forks. Angel Food Cake is best the day it is made; it becomes stale quickly (although it is wonderful toasted).

Chocolate Angel Food Cake In Step 2, substitute ¼ cup unsweetened cocoa powder for ¼ cup of the flour. (To marble the cake, make two batters, one with all flour and one with ⅛ cup cocoa substituted for ⅛ cup flour. Add the batters alternately to the tube pan, and swirl together with a knife or spatula before baking.)

Ⓥ Raspberry, Strawberry, or Other Fruit Sauce

Makes about 2 cups • Time: 5 to 10 minutes

There are many ways to make fruit sauces; the method below is one of my favorites, yielding chunky fruit in a luxurious, thick sauce. You can also create a simple sauce with more pure flavor and a very saucy consistency simply by pureeing soft fruit in a blender (then passing it through a sieve to remove seeds, if necessary). Combine with confectioners' sugar, to taste, then thin with a little water or orange or lemon juice.

½ cup water

½ cup sugar

3 tablespoons unsalted butter

2 cups berries or other ripe fruit: apples, pears, bananas, peaches, cherries, nectarines, berries, mangoes, melons, etc., picked over, pitted, peeled, washed, and/or dried, as necessary

1 Combine the water, sugar, and butter in a medium heavy-bottomed saucepan and cook over medium-high heat, shaking and stirring, until the mixture is thick and syrupy but not browned.

2 Toss in the fruit and cook over low heat until the fruit begins to break up and release its juices, about 2 minutes for berries, longer for other fruit (some fruits, such as apples, may also require the addition of a little more water). Serve warm or at room temperature. This sauce keeps well, refrigerated, for up to a week.

Chocolate Sauce

Makes about 1½ cups • Time: 15 minutes

This is a rich chocolate sauce, more substantial than syrup. It's great over fruit, ice cream, or simple cakes. Note the Hot Fudge variation.

4 ounces semisweet or bittersweet chocolate, chopped

4 tablespoons (½ stick) unsalted butter

¼ cup sugar

Pinch salt

¼ cup water

1 teaspoon vanilla extract

1 Combine all ingredients except vanilla in a small saucepan over very low heat. Cook, stirring, until the chocolate melts and the mixture is smooth.

2 Add the vanilla and serve immediately, or keep warm over hot water until ready to serve, or refrigerate for up to a week and rewarm before using.

Hot Fudge Sauce This is chewy and fudgy when you put it on top of ice cream. After the ingredients are combined, add ⅓ cup corn syrup to the mixture. Bring to a boil, turn the heat to low, and cook for 5 to 10 minutes, until thick and shiny. Add vanilla and serve hot. Or store up to a week and reheat very gently (a double boiler is best) before serving.

Butterscotch Brownies

Maybe you're allergic to chocolate, or don't like it, or are out of it. Maybe you just feel like a change. These brownies—commonly known as Blondies—will fix you right up. Add 1 cup of chocolate chips to the batter if you want to hedge a little; nuts, or any of the other ideas below, are also good.

Makes 1 to 2 dozen

Time: 30 to 40 minutes

8 tablespoons (1 stick) unsalted butter, softened, plus a little for greasing the pan

1 cup brown sugar

1 egg

1 teaspoon vanilla extract

Pinch salt

1 cup (4½ ounces) all-purpose flour

1 Preheat the oven to 350°F. Grease an 8-inch square baking pan, or line it with aluminum foil and grease the foil.

2 Melt the butter over low heat. Transfer to a bowl and use an electric mixer to beat in the brown sugar until very smooth, then beat in the egg and vanilla, stirring down the sides of the bowl every now and then.

3 Add the salt, then gently stir in the flour. Pour into the prepared pan and bake 20 to 25 minutes, or until just barely set in the middle. It's better to underbake brownies than to overbake them. Cool on a rack before cutting. Store, covered and at room temperature, for no more than a day.

5 Simple Ideas for Brownies

1 Add ½ to 1 cup chopped nuts to the batter; toast the nuts first for even better flavor.

2 Use ½ teaspoon almond or mint extract in addition to or in place of the vanilla.

3 Add ½ cup mashed bananas to the batter.

4 Add ¼ cup bourbon, scotch, or other whisky to the batter; increase the flour by 1 tablespoon.

5 Stir ½ cup dried fruit, especially dried cherries, into the prepared batter.

Rice Pudding

This simple, no-egg rice pudding is sweet and easy.

Makes 8 servings

Time: 40 minutes

2 cups water

1 cup long- or short-grain rice

Dash salt

2 cups milk

¾ cup sugar, or more to taste

1 teaspoon ground cinnamon
or cardamom

1 Bring the water to a boil in a medium saucepan; stir in the rice and the salt. Cover and cook over low heat until almost all the water is absorbed, about 20 minutes.

2 Uncover, pour in the milk and cook, stirring frequently, until about half the milk is absorbed. Stir in the sugar and spices and continue to cook until the rice is very soft and the milk absorbed. About halfway through cooking, taste and add more sugar if necessary.

3 Spoon into custard cups and serve warm or cold, garnished with whipped cream if you like. This keeps well for 2 days or more, covered and refrigerated.

5 Simple Ideas for Rice Pudding

1 Add ¼ cup or more raisins, or snipped dates, figs, or other dried fruit about halfway through the cooking.

2 Use Fresh Coconut Milk (page 79) or canned coconut milk in place of some or all of the milk.

3 Add 1 teaspoon of vanilla extract, orange blossom, or rose water at the end of cooking.

4 Add 1 teaspoon minced lemon or orange zest in place of spices.

6 Garnish with a sprinkling of toasted sliced almonds or other nuts.

Vegetarian Menus

Vegan Recipes

Tips Reference

Here's an at-a-glance reference of the tips in this book. If you're ever looking for some quick info—on mushrooms, for example—you can look here, instead of scanning the index and flipping through recipe pages trying to find it. The page reference leads you back to the related recipe, if you want to consult it.

Asparagus   Asparagus size is a matter of debate; some people prefer super-thin stalks, which need not be peeled, a distinct advantage. But big, fat stalks are great to eat, too. My recommendation: Take what you get. Don't buy shriveled spears or damaged ones; and don't buy canned or frozen asparagus. *See page 89.*

    Store asparagus, wrapped loosely in plastic, in the refrigerator. Use as soon as possible. *See page 89.*

Avocados   You can buy avocados hard, and they will ripen nicely on your kitchen counter. Don't buy them if they're super-mushy or have bruises, and always handle them gently. *See page 2.*

    Cut an avocado in half from pole to pole. If you want to store half, wrap it with the pit intact and refrigerate it that way; this will keep it from turning brown. *See page 2.*

Barley   Almost all barley is pearled—its hard outer husk is removed—but whole barley is sold in many health food stores. Be sure you know what you're getting; whole barley takes a couple of hours to cook, and never becomes completely tender. *See page 27.*

Bean sprouts   Bean sprouts should be stored in the refrigerator. Eat them within a few days. *See page 55.*

    If you have a few days, you can make your own bean sprouts: Rinse $1/2$ cup whole mung beans with water, then soak for 6 to 12 hours. Put in a jar or bowl that you can cover with a piece of cheesecloth or a very coarse napkin. Drain, rinse, and drain them again. Prop the jar up so that it is on its side with the mouth tilted down. Shield from the light with the cheesecloth. Rinse and drain at least twice a day. After a couple of days, the seeds will have sprouted. When the sprouts are the length you want them, rinse one more time and expose to the light for a few hours; this will turn the sprouts green. *See page 55.*

Beans   There is a difference between fresh and stale beans: newer beans taste better, cook faster, and contain more nutrients. Go to a place where there is a fair amount of turnover—a natural foods store, for example, or a Latin market. Your supermarket may sell a lot of beans these days, so you might start there, but if it seems that the beans you buy take longer to cook than you might expect given my guidelines, try buying them elsewhere. *See page 73.*

    Generally, beans should look consistent, and have deep, somewhat glossy color; faded, dry-looking beans are likely to be older, and those that are starting to wrinkle are not worth buying. *See page 73.*

    Store beans in covered containers or thick plastic bags in a dry place. I finish all the beans I've accumulated during the course of the year each summer, so that I know that I don't keep any longer than a year. *See page 73.*

    Sort through beans just before soaking or cooking: Put the beans in a pot and fill it with water, then swish the whole thing around while looking into the pot. Remove any beans that are discolored, shriveled, or broken and remove any pebbles or other stray matter. Then dump the beans into a colander and rinse for a minute or so. *See page 73.*

    Salt beans halfway through cooking, after they have begun to tenderize. Don't wait until they are done to add salt or they will be bland. *See page 73.*

Beets Beets grow spring through fall, but are available pretty much year-round. Size doesn't matter—large beets are easier to handle, and only rarely become woody. Don't buy them if they're mushy. One good indication of freshness is the presence of greens. *See page 90.*

To store beets, remove all but an inch of the greens (use them immediately), and place the roots in a plastic bag in the refrigerator. They keep for weeks. *See page 90.*

Scrub beets well before cooking, but leave an inch or so of the green tops on to minimize bleeding. *See page 90.*

When you can easily pierce a beet with a skewer or thin-bladed knife, it's done. Slight overcooking is usually preferable to undercooking. *See page 90.*

Blue cheese Blue cheese can be made from the milk of goats, cows, or sheep. Goat blue has the distinctive flavor associated with all goat cheeses, and tends to be less creamy than the other two. The best known blue sheep cheese is Roquefort. Usually, however, it's easier to find a good Gorgonzola or Stilton (both made from cow's milk), or a good domestic variety, like Maytag blue. Good blue cheese should be quite soft, though not runny. *See page 19.*

Broccoli To prepare broccoli, strip the stalk of leaves, if any (these can be cooked along with the tops and eaten, if you like). Remove the bottom inch of the stalk, or wherever it has dried out. Peel the tough outer skin of the broccoli stalk with a paring knife or vegetable peeler. (To peel with a paring knife, hold the broccoli upside down; grasp a bit of the skin right at the bottom, between the paring knife and your thumb. Pull down to remove a strip of the skin.) If you like, cut the stalk into equal-length pieces and break the head into florets. *See page 31.*

Bulgur Bulgur comes in four grinds: *Fine* (Number 1) is almost always just soaked rather than cooked. *Medium* (Number 2) can be soaked or cooked. *Coarse* (Number 3) must be cooked. *Very coarse* (Number 4) you won't see often. Most supermarkets stock medium, which you can consider all-purpose if you like. Fine-grind and coarse can be found in many natural foods stores, specialty food markets, and Middle Eastern stores. *See page 23.*

Cabbage Cabbage is a year-round vegetable, widely shipped and found locally when the weather is cool. Reject any cabbages with yellow, soft, or loose leaves. *See page 17.*

All head cabbage, regardless of color, as well as napa cabbage, should be cored before cooking or shredding. First remove a couple of layers of the outer leaves. Then use a thin-bladed knife to cut a cone-shaped section out of the core, making the wide end of the cone a circle about 1/2 inch wider than the core itself. *See page 17.*

To shred head cabbage, just cut the cabbage into quarters (or eighths, if it is large), and cross-cut thinly; it will shred itself. To shred napa cabbage, just cross-cut; no quartering is necessary. *See page 17.*

Chiles Fresh chiles are tricky, because it's hard to predict how hot they'll be. Generally, it's best to remove seeds (the hottest part), and then taste a little piece before deciding how much to add. Wear rubber gloves when working with chiles, or wash your hands very well as soon as you're done handling them. *See page 2.*

Dumplings   Supermarkets usually stock both square and round wonton wrappers; either can be frozen for later use. Square wrappers are a little easier to handle, but round ones yield a less doughy dumpling; the choice is yours. *See page 10.*

Eggplants   Eggplant need not be peeled unless the skin is very thick, or, of course, unless you prefer to do so. *See page 94.*

It's usually worth salting larger eggplant, a process which draws out excess moisture and a certain amount of bitterness along with it. Trim off the ends, then cut it into slices (you can cut long slices or crosswise ones) from $1/2$ to 1 inch thick. Or cut it into chunks. Sprinkle both sides of the slices (or all sides of the chunks) liberally with coarse salt, then let drain in a colander for at least half an hour, or up to 2 hours. Rinse and squeeze dry between paper or cloth towels. *See page 94.*

Fennel   With fennel, (also called anise), you're primarily interested in the bulb, not the stalks. It should be tight and greenish white, with little or no browning or shriveled parts. Store fennel, loosely wrapped, in the vegetable bin, for up to a week—but use it as soon as you can. *See page 18.*

Trim fennel's feathery fronds and hollow stalks; use them for seasoning or discard. Trim off the hard bottom and cut vertical slices through the bulb. Or cut in half, dig out the core, and cut into thin strips to then dice for salads, or for sautéing, braising, or roasting (but not grilling, when you need larger pieces). *See page 18.*

Grains   Most grains, even when processed to remove their hulls, or lightly precooked in the traditional style (as are bulgur and kasha), retain most of their natural oils, so buying them as fresh as possible is key to avoiding rancidity. Buy them in bulk, from a place with fast turnover. That may mean a specialty store (for instance, you can get great bulgur in a Middle Eastern store) or a natural foods store. *See page 58.*

You can store grains in the refrigerator, but if there is room in the freezer, that's even better; there's no need to defrost before cooking. *See page 58.*

Most grains (bulgur and kasha are the exceptions) should be rinsed before cooking. *See page 58.*

Immersion blender   An immersion blender is basically a stick with a blender blade on the end of it. It was created to puree large quantities of soups in restaurants while they remained in the pot. Models designed for home use are not nearly as powerful as regular blenders, but they make creaming soups less labor intensive and messy than using a standard blender. *See page 31.*

Kale   Kale, like collards—its close, non-crinkly relative—has large, dark green, almost leathery leaves. But both greens (and they are interchangeable) are at their sweetest when grown in cool weather. *See page 28.*

Kale and collards   There's only one trick to cooking kale and collards: Make sure you cook them long enough to soften the stems. Undercooked stems are unpleasantly tough and chewy. (One sure way to prevent this is to avoid collards with stems more than $1/8$ inch thick.) *See page 28.*

Lentils Ordinary lentils may be greenish brown or brownish green, but the best are dark green, and are originally from France. Called *lentilles de Puy,* they're smaller than most, and they remain firm throughout cooking, never becoming quite as mushy as the others. *See page 34.*

When using lentils in soup, it's best to remove about half of them, puree them, and then return them to the pot, giving you a wonderful texture of half puree, half firm lentils. *See page 34.*

Mushrooms To trim mushrooms, cut off any hard or dried-out spots—usually just the end of the stem. The stems of most mushrooms are perfectly edible (those of shiitakes are not, but they can be used for stock). Rinse off any dirt in running water, but quickly, or the mushrooms may become waterlogged. *See page 96.*

Olive oil Olive oil is really the only all-purpose oil, and it's become increasingly easy to buy. The best is extra-virgin oil; technically it's defined by the amount of acid it contains, but you can think of it simply as the first, cold pressing of olives. There are no chemicals used in this process and the result, more often than not, is oil of distinctively fine character. It can be very expensive—$20 liter bottles are not uncommon—but it can also be reasonably priced at about $20 a gallon. *See page 48.*

Pasta A pasta and bean soup might traditionally be made with leftover bits of pasta—the ends of a number of boxes in the pantry. This is a good idea, just don't overdo it. Too much pasta will make the soup way too starchy—and if you're using long or big pasta, break it up before cooking. *See page 35.*

There are times when the shape of pasta matters and times when it does not. Tiny morsels, for example, such as orzo, tubetti, and ditalini, are best in soups, because they fit on a spoon. Long pastas, like spaghetti and linguine, are best with sauces that don't have large chunks in them. Sauces with chunks should be served with bigger, tube-shaped pasta, such as penne, rigatoni, or ziti, or with shells and elbows. You shouldn't change the type of sauce you're making because you don't have the "correct" pasta shape. If you make spaghetti with a chunky sauce, some of the sauce will stay at the bottom of the bowl. This is less than ideal, of course, but you can eat that sauce with a spoon, or some bread. *See page 44.*

Peppers Yellow and orange peppers seem to be mellowest, but they're usually expensive, so red is the common first choice, green last. Avoid peppers with soft spots or bruises, or those that feel very full—since you buy them by weight, there's no need to pay for lots of seeds. Store peppers, unwrapped, in the vegetable bin, for a week or so. *See page 5.*

Pumpkin or squash You can make pumpkin or squash soup without garlic or bread. In fact, combining squash with water or stock and seasonings, then pureeing, produces a soup that is so creamy it's hard to believe it has no dairy. For extra thickness, you can stir in some milk, cream, sour cream, or yogurt. Another good addition is roasted (or boiled) and chopped chestnuts, or sliced and quickly browned apples. *See page 32.*

Quesadillas Cheddar and "jack" cheese are very much alike, and are both best in their sharper (that is, well-aged) forms. If you want authentic taste, the best cheese for quesadillas, and one that is becoming more widely available (especially in cities with a large Hispanic population) is *quesillo* (or queso Oaxaca), which is like mozzarella. This, mixed with cheddar or the similar *queso chilmalma*, makes for the ideal quesadilla. *See page 8.*

Polenta Many Italian stores and supermarkets sell instant polenta, which is easy to make—and not bad, but not great. Short on taste, too, are the mass-produced commercial cornmeals sold in supermarkets, although "stone-ground" cornmeal sold in the baking aisles can be good. I recommend fresh stone-ground cornmeal from a natural foods store; store it in the freezer. Medium-grind cornmeal is best for both flavor and texture; although it takes a little longer to cook, it's worth the time. *See page 67.*

Rice There are essentially two kinds of rice: long and short grain. Long-grain rice cooks in separate, firm, dry kernels; short-grain (and so-called medium-grain) rice cooks up soft, moist, and a little sticky. Basmati is the best tasting long-grain specialty rice. Jasmine rice is also long grain, and also aromatic. But it cooks as if it were short grain; that is, moist and somewhat sticky. It has a wonderful aroma and flavor, and is associated with Thai food. *See page 60.*

Saffron There is real and fake saffron, the former from crocuses, the latter from marigolds. The difference is in cost and taste, and though real saffron is expensive, it's worth it. And, as it turns out, it isn't all that expensive per use. Buy an ounce from a reputable spice dealer for about $35 and if you use it wisely, it will last you five years. *See page 45.*

Spices Whole spices keep longer and, once ground, have more intense flavor than pre-ground spices. Generally speaking, it's best to toast them before grinding—just cook them in a dry skillet until they become fragrant, a couple of minutes—then grind in a spice or coffee grinder. *See page 68.*

Squash To prepare hard-skinned squashes, use a cleaver or very large knife to split the squash in half. Scoop out the seeds and strings and discard (or bake the seeds as you would Fiery Pumpkin Seeds, page 33). Peeling butternut squash is fairly easy, as long as you have a sturdy vegetable peeler or a paring knife. Peeling acorn and other odd-shaped squash is virtually impossible, so don't try. *See page 100.*

Winter squash gets sweeter later in the season; November and December's squashes are more delicious than those from early fall. Though the flesh of all of them is roughly equivalent, I buy butternut squash because it's easiest to peel—use a paring knife, and don't worry too much about precision. *See page 32.*

Tofu Tofu is usually sold as being one of four textures; these are relative rather than absolute terms, but worth noting: Silken: Best for soups, to puree for use in sauces, or to fry; Soft: As soft as silken but also can be pressed, frozen, or marinated and cooked on its own; Firm: Good for stir-fries, can be marinated, pressed, or frozen; Extra-firm: Best for stir-fries. *See page 85.*

Even though most tofu is packaged (in a small tub filled with water, then wrapped in plastic), it's best to use it as soon as you buy it. If you don't use it all at once, place the remainder in a plastic or glass container, cover it with fresh water, and seal tightly. Change the water daily. *See page 85.*

To press tofu (to make it firmer): Cut a brick of tofu in half through its equator. Place each half on a cutting board and prop the board up so that its lower end is at the edge of a sink. Top with another cutting board or similar flat, clean object. Weight the top board with a skillet, a couple of books, whatever. Let sit for 30 to 60 minutes, then drain on paper towels. *See page 85.*

Index

Conversions, Substitutions, and Helpful Hints

Cooking at High Altitudes

Every increase in elevation brings a decrease in air pressure, which results in a lower boiling point. At 7,000 feet, for example—the altitude of many towns in the Southwest—water boils at 199°F. This means slower cooking times (and makes a pressure cooker a more desirable appliance). Families who have been
living in the mountains for years have already discovered, though trial and error, the best ways to adjust.

Newcomers to high altitudes must be patient and experiment to discover what works best. But here are some general rules for high-altitude cooking:

1. For stove-top cooking, use higher heat when practical; extend cooking times as necessary. Beans and grains will require significantly more time than at sea level.

2. Assume that batters and doughs will rise faster than at sea level.

3. Over 3,000 feet, increase baking temperatures by 25°F.

4. Over 3,000 feet, reduce baking powder (or other leavening) measurements by about ten percent; increase liquid in baked goods by the same percentage. You may want to reduce the amount of sugar slightly as well.

5. For every 2,000 foot increase in altitude above 3,000 feet, reduce leavening even further.

Imperial Measurements

Theoretically, both the United Kingdom and Canada use the metric system, but older recipes rely on the "imperial" measurement system, which differs from standard U.S. measurements in its liquid ("fluid") measurements:

$1/4$ cup = 2.5 ounces

$1/2$ cup ("gill") = 5 ounces

1 cup = 10 ounces

1 pint = 20 ounces

1 quart = 40 ounces

Some Useful Substitutions

1 cup cake flour = $7/8$ cup all-purpose flour + $1/8$ cup cornstarch

1 tablespoon baking powder = 2 teaspoons baking soda + 1 teaspoon cream of tartar

1 cup buttermilk = 1 scant cup milk at room temperature + 1 tablespoon white vinegar

1 cup brown sugar = 1 cup white sugar + 2 tablespoons molasses

1 cup sour cream = 1 cup yogurt (preferably full fat)

Measurement Conversions

Note that volume (i.e., cup) measures and weight (i.e., ounce) measures convert perfectly for liquids only. Solids are a different story; 1 cup of flour weighs only 4 or 5 ounces.

Dash or pinch = less than $1/4$ teaspoon

3 teaspoons = 1 tablespoon

2 tablespoons = 1 fluid ounce

4 tablespoons = $1/4$ cup = 2 fluid ounces

16 tablespoons = 1 cup = 8 fluid ounces

2 cups = 1 pint

2 pints = 1 quart

4 quarts = 1 gallon

Imperial vs. Metric

These are approximate, but are fine for all uses.

1 ounce = 28 grams

1 pound = 500 grams or $1/2$ kilo

2.2 pounds = 1 kilo

1 teaspoon = 5 milliliters (ml)

1 tablespoon = 15 milliliters

1 cup = $1/4$ liter

1 quart = 1 liter